Deborah Manley edits educational books, mainly for the developing world. She trained for social work, but was only briefly employed in that field. Since she was a student she has lived in London, apart from several years in Nigeria, where her husband was teaching. She has written two books, one on careers in Nigeria, and the other an anthology of West African childhood memories. She has two children.

Pamela Royds was born in London and after periods spent in Oxford, East Anglia, Calcutta and Bombay, she returned to London where she lives with her journalist husband and four children. For the past seven years she has worked as an editor of children's books.

Nancy Tuft was born in Liverpool and is a professional journalist contributing feature articles to the *Daily Telegraph Magazine, Nova, The Times* and many other newspapers. She is married to Leslie Tuft, who is a writer and social services adviser, and they live in Notting Hill Gate with their three children. Strongly influenced by Merseyside's vivid culture, she is appalled at how little use Londoners make of the resources of their city.

USING LONDON

Deborah Manley
Pamela Royds
Nancy Tuft

Penguin Books

Penguin Books Ltd, Harmondsworth,
Middlesex, England
Penguin Books Inc., 7110 Ambassador Road,
Baltimore, Maryland 21207, U.S.A.
Penguin Books Australia Ltd, Ringwood,
Victoria, Australia

First published in paperback by Penguin Books and in hardback by
André Deutsch 1971
Copyright © Deborah Manley, Pamela Royds, Nancy Tuft, 1971

Made and printed in Great Britain by
Hazell Watson & Viney Ltd,
Aylesbury, Bucks
Set in Monotype Times

CONTENTS

INTRODUCTION

Using London is a handbook for people living in London or coming to live in London. It is not a guide for visitors or tourists, though there is much in it which would make their stay more valuable.

You can be lonely and bored in London. You can live in one of the world's most exciting cities and know next to nothing of its excitement. Yet, just round the corner, other people may be doing just the things you want to do. How do you get to know what is going on? We hope this book will help to tell you. *Using London* is not, however, comprehensive, it cannot be, there's too much happening and things change too fast. On one underground station we once counted three hundred separate advertised events: films, concerts, plays, classes, fairs, outings, exhibitions, sporting events and happenings. So we have had to be selective. In doing this we have picked out established, but by no means establishment, organizations and listed regular rather than ephemeral events. We have also concentrated on organizations asking for active participation rather than dormant membership.

But it's not only what you can do that is important. People coming Dick Whittington-wise to London bring their problems and their basic personalities with them. They come to find themselves and their fortunes and often get lost in the process. They may be living away from home for the first time. They have to make their own decisions and learn through their mistakes. Sometimes living in London can seem like a big mistake. But it's a big enough place to be able to pick up the pieces and start all over again. To help with this *Using London* lists many of the agencies that deal with or give advice on all types of personal problems; not that they have a pre-packaged answer to every human dilemma – people must find the ultimate solutions to their difficulties themselves – but there is an enormous amount of help available for those who want it.

And sometimes you'll want to get out of London. Even this can lead to more links within London if you get involved with some of the organizations listed in the 'Getting Away' chapter.

The real point then of *Using London* is to give you contacts and leads. Its value will be shown by your use of them.

Finally, all the information given in the book is, to the best of our knowledge, correct at the time of going to press. When this book was being written admission charges to museums were under discussion. We have let 'admission free' stand – hopefully. If anyone feels that they have been misrepresented or if anyone feels they should have been included on the basis of our selection criteria, we would be pleased to hear from them.

A ROOF OVER YOUR HEAD

EMERGENCY ACCOMMODATION

For emergency crash pads try the following:
BIT [229 – 8219].
STUDENT ADVISORY CENTRE [402 – 5233].

If you're stranded in London without money for a bed at night, try the local office of the SUPPLEMENTARY BENEFITS COMMISSION, the address of which can be obtained from the nearest post office. You must apply in person, not by telephone, and they will consider your application. Students on grants and non-British residents are not normally eligible for help. These local area-offices close at 4 p.m. and are not open on Saturdays. The Emergency Office of the Supplementary Benefits Commission, 96 Great Guildford Street, SE1 [928 – 6870] opens till 10 p.m. including Sundays and Public Holidays.

Girls without cash might try the Women's Reception Centre, the only one in the country for women, run by the Supplementary Benefits Commission at Great Guildford Street. This isn't a hostel. They have a statutory function to provide overnight accommodation for women 'without a settled way of life'. It is dormitory accommodation but better furnished than a lot of hostels. It's warmer than the Embankment on a wet night and they have TV. They will only take you in if you have no money and if they have a bed available.

CHURCH ARMY EMERGENCY HOSTEL, 1–3 Cosway Street, NW1 [262 – 3818]. For girls only.

CHEAP, TEMPORARY ACCOMMODATION

The problem of finding cheap, temporary accommodation in London for a few days is acute, particularly in the summer months. Always book in advance whenever possible.

THE YOUTH HOTEL, Hyde House, 9 Bulstrode Street, W1 [935 – 7887] which is run by the YWCA, has dormitory accommodation for young men and women.

VANDON HOUSE, 1 Vandon Street, SW1 [799 – 6780] is a cheap hotel for both sexes run by the Salvation Army.

DEVONSHIRE STREET HOUSE, 30 Devonshire Street, London W1N 2AP [935 – 7817] is a residential centre which is also the headquarters of the National Association of Youth Clubs. Residential amenities are available to all members of clubs affiliated to the National Association of Youth Clubs and adults associated with these clubs. Other young people and adults, especially those connected with educational and youth services in this country and abroad, are welcome to stay when accommodation is available. Bedrooms are single, double and three-bedded, and two rooms have six beds. Party bookings are accepted, provided the leader is at least 21. Meals are available in the restaurant seven days a week. The house is specially designed to cater for physically handicapped people. The entrance to the building is completely flat, thus enabling easy access for wheelchairs, and there is a lift to all floors. Garage space is sometimes available, 25p per day.

Accommodation is only on a short-term basis and usually bookings can only be taken for five to seven days. Single rooms for affiliated guests, £1·60 per night; non-affiliated guests, £2·10. Shared rooms are slightly cheaper.

THE IRISH CENTRE, 52 Camden Square, NW1 [485 – 0051/2] offers a temporary home to fellow countrymen and women (aged 16–25) while finding their feet in London. It has a male and female hostel as well as a social centre and welfare workers to help with jobs and any other problems.

YHA HOSTELS. There are three youth hostels in London for members of the YHA (see p. 183 for details of membership):

Holland House, Holland Walk, W8 [937 – 0748].
84 Highgate West Hill, N6 [340 – 1831].
38 Bolton Gardens, SW5 [373 – 7083].
Maximum stay is three nights.

CARAVAN HARBOUR, North Parade, Crystal Palace Camping Site, SE19 [778 – 7155] is for people with their own caravan, motorized caravan, or tent. Hot water, showers, wash-basins and washing lines are available, as well as a shop for groceries. It is essential to book ahead for July and August. Normal camping charges.

FOR VISITORS

HOTAC, 93 Baker Street, W1 [935 – 2555] is a hotel accommodation service which saves the time-consuming business of ringing hotel after hotel in order to find a vacancy. Ring Hotac, tell them your price range (£2 per night for a single and £3·75 for a double is their minimum) and they will find and book a hotel room for you. You settle your own hotel bill and there is no reservation charge for people in London or abroad. Otherwise a fee of 15p per person is payable on application. They do advance reservations as well as an 'Instant Reservation' service for the same night.

For visitors arriving in London there is a free direct telephone-link to Hotac located at Victoria Station in the General Inquiry office, opposite platform nine, and at Waterloo Station in the concourse, next to the post office. This operates weekdays from 10 a.m. to 10 p.m. from May till October, and the rest of the year from 10 a.m. to 6 p.m. including all Saturdays.

Besides Hotac, the following hotel booking agencies provide a free service in London:

HOTEL BOOKINGS INTERNATIONAL, Sutherland House, 5/6 Argyll Street, W1 [734 – 7381].

HOTEL GUIDE, Faraday House, 8–10 Charing Cross Road, WC2 [836 – 5561].

ROSENTHAL HOTEL BOOKING SERVICE, 190 Shaftesbury Avenue, WC2 [628 – 8202].

THE LONDON TOURIST BOARD, has an accommodation ser-vice at 4 Grosvenor Gardens, SW1 [629 – 5414] and information bureaux at Arrivals Hall, BOAC Terminal, Buckingham Palace Road, SW1, and British Rail Enquiry Office, opposite platform nine, Victoria Station, SW1. Postal inquiries are dealt with and provisional arrangements for suitable accommodation will be made free of charge.

HOSTELS

Hostel life has its restrictions. You may have to share a room, and you may have to be in by a certain time at night. You mightn't feel free to ask your friends back. But a hostel does have certain advantages and does provide a cheap base while you look round for a flat of your own, or find someone to share a flat with. And there are usually mod. cons. laid on like baths and showers and laundry facilities.

Hostel accommodation should be booked well in advance as there are waiting lists. Ideally, as soon as you know when you are coming to London you should start making arrangements because of the scarcity of accommodation.

THE YWCA ACCOMMODATION AND ADVISORY SERVICE, 16 Great Russell Street, WC1 [580 – 0478] publishes (in conjunction with the London Council for the Welfare of Women and Girls) a booklet (price 20p) giving the addresses of a wide range of wo-men's accommodation of all kinds, not only YWs. Not all these addresses are hostels. Some are bedsitters with a communal kitchen. They also have a list of private landladies who let bedsitters in their houses. The interviewing hours for this intro-ductory service to landladies are 12 a.m. to 4 p.m., Monday to Friday. They also run a counselling service two nights a week on Tuesdays and Thursdays from 7 to 8.30 p.m. for girls in difficulty.

The YMCA Divisional Office, 37 Bedford Square, WC1 [636 – 3742] will send on request a list of both temporary and permanent hostels for men. Application for accommodation should be made direct to the individual hostel.

GLC HOSTELS. The GLC has some hostel accommodation for

persons employed, training or studying in London. Men: 47 Milman's Street, SW10; 7 Woodfield Road, W9; 43 Holmes Road, NW5. Women: 22a Craven Hill Gardens, W2; St George's Hostel, 47 Milman's Street, SW10. Applications for these should be made to the Director of Housing, County Hall, Westminster Bridge, SE1 [928 – 5000].

LONDON HOSTELS ASSOCIATION, 51 Warwick Square, SW1 [834 – 1545, Accommodation 828 – 3263]. This is a non-profit-making association, providing accommodation in twenty-five hostels, mainly for young office workers. Priority is given to civil servants but there are usually vacancies for others, though few in single rooms. There is no married accommodation. Applicants should apply to the head office for details, not more than one month in advance. There are two leaflets which you can send for, one giving details of residential accommodation, and another listing temporary accommodation for visitors.

BEDSITTERS AND FLATS

A halfway arrangement between a hostel and a flat is to be a paying guest in someone's home.

UNIVERSAL AUNTS, 36 Walpole Street, SW3 [730 – 9834] have an introductory service. They also have furnished flats.

RENTAGUEST, 110 Horseferry Road, SW1 [222 – 1664] offers a personal service supplying details of rooms available in private houses, both where meals are provided and where you do your own catering. They also have furnished flats and bedsitters.

Two old-established agencies for flats are RAMBLERS OF LONDON LTD, 24 Ashburn Place, SW7 [370 – 1528] (plus at least half a dozen other phone numbers listed in the book) and WASPS AND CO., 40 Beauchamp Place, SW3 [584 – 6863].

The Times, the *Daily Telegraph*, local London papers as well as London's two evening papers, the *Standard* and the *Evening News*, which publish early-morning editions, have flats to let in their classified ads. Go after these immediately if you like the sound of any. Be careful of flat-letting agencies who charge a huge commission and who don't vet the accommodation. Agencies very often put private ads. in the paper, so be careful. Premiums are illegal under the Rent Act.

You may be lucky and find a room or flat advertised in the window of a newsagent's shop, particularly around Earls Court, Notting Hill Gate, Camden or Brixton.

It saves fares and travelling time if you confine your search to one area. Before deciding which area of London appeals to you, and they all have their own character and flavour, it's worth bearing in mind that rents are much higher in areas like Kensington, Chelsea, Hampstead. It's no accident either that areas like these, with an abnormally high ratio of people living alone in bedsitters, have a suicide rate which is twice the national average. It can be very easy for a person living alone to get lonely, then depressed and isolated, and to think it's all due to his or her own inadequacy. Some people *can* live self-sufficiently on their own. Others need companionship. So if you're just starting to live in London, away from your family, it's well worth making an effort to find a number of compatible people to share with. An added advantage in sharing a flat is that you can also share facilities like TV, fridge and cooker which you mightn't normally get in a bedsitter. It is important in any sharing arrangement to sort out early on who does what about cooking, cleaning, shopping, entertaining, etc., because these can be frequent sources of friction between people who otherwise started off as good friends.

There are a number of flat-sharing agencies who will introduce you to other people wanting a third, fourth or fifth person to share with. Their aim is to fix people up with flat-mates of similar sex, age, interests and backgrounds. Usually the charge for this introduction is your share of the first week's rent.

FLAT-SHARE, 213 Piccadilly, W1 [734 – 0318].

FLATSHARERS REGISTER, 11 Beauchamp Place, SW3 [584 – 0395 and 0232].

SHARE-A-FLAT, 175 Piccadilly, W1 [493 – 2545].

COMMUNES

The ultimate in sharing is to join a commune. Joining a commune however involves a deep commitment and is far more than just somewhere to live. It means a whole re-orientation of attitudes. Communes vary. In some, people have outside jobs and feed their income into the commune. In others, the involvement is more total and the people work within the commune itself, making clothes and looking after their immediate physical needs. Some welcome outsiders; others are closed communities. Some specify the sort of person they are looking for dependent on the contribution that person can make to the commune.

BIT, 141 Westbourne Park Road, W11 [229 – 8219] publishes a directory of communes (15p plus postage), which lists communes in this country and Europe, as well as those in London. Also from Bit you can get a copy of the magazine of the whole commune movement which comes out every two months (15p plus postage).

Regular festivals of communes held every six months or so provide an opportunity for outsiders to find out more about them, and to meet the people who live in them.

TROUBLE WITH THE LANDLORD

If you need advice before signing a lease, or have trouble with the landlord go to the nearest CITIZENS' ADVICE BUREAU. A list of local offices is given in the phone book. You don't need an appointment, just walk in. The CAB will help you to sort out the intricacies of the Rent Act and can explain the technical differences between furnished and unfurnished accommodation, the principal difference being that there is far less security of tenure with furnished accommodation.

If you feel you are paying too high a rent, the CAB will advise you about contacting the local Rent Officer, or the Rent Tribunal in the case of furnished accommodation. Be careful here. There's no point in applying for a rent reduction on a furnished flat if it means that the landlord will only retaliate by taking out an eviction order in six months' time.

In the case of an unfurnished flat there is a Register of Fair Rents in the Rent Officer's department at your local town hall, freely available for inspection by the public. So you can compare what you are paying with rents of flats in comparable properties in the same neighbourhood which have already been assessed under the Rent Act. There's all the difference in the world between a fair rent and a market rent.

LAMBETH HOUSING ADVICE CENTRE, Borough of Lambeth, Town Hall Parade, Brixton Hill, SW2 [274 – 7722].

This unique housing information service will help anyone in Lambeth who has a housing problem: private house-owners, or tenants and potential ones; as well as Council tenants. If you want a mortgage or an improvement grant, or wish to move to a new town, they will give individual advice in a private glass-partitioned interviewing room.

SETTLING DOWN

THE HOUSING CORPORATION, which has its South-East Regional Office at 122 King's Road, SW3 [589 – 8201], was set up by the Government to stimulate the Housing Society movement. Its business is to encourage Housing Societies to build new homes to be let at non-profit rents or on a co-ownership basis.

A cost-rent society is in effect a non-profit-making landlord which provides houses or flats for letting on tenancies or leases. You get good value for money plus the freedom to move at short notice, usually one month.

A co-ownership society provides houses or flats to be occupied exclusively by its members. As shareholders in the Society they collectively own the dwellings which they occupy individually under a tenancy agreement or lease. The cash outlay is a lot less than the deposit, legal costs and surveyor's fees normally needed by owner-occupiers and there are no worries about getting a mortgage. The Society borrows on its collective credit and loans are repayable over forty years. The great advantage is that on leaving, if he has occupied his home for at least five years, a member gets back a proportion of the rent he has paid.

The Housing Corporation publishes a Directory of Cost-rent and Co-ownership housing-schemes, which includes a section on Greater London. Accommodation ranges from bedsitters to four-bedroomed flats and houses.

SHELTER HOUSING AID CENTRE, 1a The Boltons, SW10 [373 – 7276]. SHAC gives advice to engaged and married couples as well as families. It has a department dealing specifically with house purchase. They are able to name those building societies which take a wife's earnings into consideration, as well as overtime earnings. They can tell you too which building societies will grant mortgages on older properties. Ring or write for an appointment, and tell them what the situation is so that they can fix the appointment with a person most likely to be able to help you.

Some useful books are *A Home of Your Own* (12½p), published by Shelter, 86 The Strand, WC2, in which the complications of house purchase are set out in simple terms; *The Legal Side of Buying a House* (50p), a *Which?* Supplement published by the Consumers' Association, Caxton Hill, Hertford; and *Buying a House* (25p), a Penguin Handbook.

ACCOMMODATION AND HOSPITALITY FOR OVERSEAS STUDENTS AND VISITORS

THE BRITISH TOURIST AUTHORITY, 64 St James Street, SW1 [629 – 9191] provides information on accommodation for both individuals and parties. A booklet called *London – A Guide to Inexpensive Accommodation* is available from them here in this country and from their offices abroad. Also available from the BTA is a booklet, published by the Central Bureau for Educational Visits and Exchanges, called *Young Visitors to Britain*. This comes out every spring in French, German and Spanish as well as in English. It gives information on accommodation, social contacts and welfare, holiday and study arrangements.

LONDON TOURIST BOARD. Accommodation service at 4 Grosvenor Gardens, SW1 [629 – 5414] (see p. 12).

OVERSEAS VISITORS' CLUB, 3 Templeton Place, Earls Court, SW5 [373 – 6066] is a few minutes' away from Earls Court underground station and five minutes' walk from the West London Air Terminal. They will arrange hotel bookings in the immediate vicinity. There is a baggage store, a mail-forwarding service, an employment bureau, and an accommodation bureau for people wanting longer-stay accommodation. There are general inquiry services and amenities for overseas visitors.

THE BRITISH COUNCIL STUDENTS' CENTRE, 11 Portland Place, W1 [636 – 6888]. Centre membership (annual £1·50; per term 75p) is open to all full-time students from abroad; a lively programme of social and cultural activities is offered (including remedial English classes, day and weekend study visits, holiday courses, etc.). The Centre is open seven days a week and welcomes British as well as overseas members. Restaurant bar, TV, games and study facilities are available. It also provides arrival and accommodation services for those on officially administered awards or recommended through High Commissions or embassies. Hospitality in British homes is arranged for overseas students and advisory services assist with information about clubs and organizations throughout London.

INTERNATIONAL FRIENDSHIP LEAGUE, Peacehaven, Creswick Road, W3 [992 – 0221] has temporary as well as long-term accommodation for visitors and students of all nationalities. Also TV-lounge and library, large garden, dancing and games room.

INTERNATIONAL HOUSE, 40 Shaftesbury Avenue, W1 [437 – 9167] arranges residential accommodation in private houses and hostels. It also has an information and welfare bureau, a students' club and travel and employment bureaux. At the same address is the International Language Centre with language courses and a teacher training institute.

INTERNATIONAL STUDENTS' HOUSE, 1–6 Park Crescent, W1 [636 – 9472] has a restaurant, bar, coffee-bar, and a programme of social activities as well as residential accommodation. It is open every day of the year and has an information bureau which will advise about courses and cheap travel, as well as accommodation.

TRUMAN & KNIGHTLEY EDUCATIONAL TRUST, 91/93 Baker Street, W1 [486 – 0931] will put overseas students in touch with first-class language schools (for English) who can also offer accommodation in and around London. There is no charge for this service.

THE GABBITAS-THRING EDUCATIONAL TRUST LTD, 6 Sackville Street, W1 [734–0161] has a similar advisory service.

THE AFRICA CENTRE, 38 King Street, Covent Garden, WC2 [836 – 1973] has a combined programme of educational and social activities. Besides holding information and discussion forums on all aspects of contemporary life in Africa, there are exhibitions, recitals and films. Evening classes are available in French, Arabic, and Swahili and there is a special Women's Programme offering a certificate course in community studies, which gives an understanding of social change in Africa.

The Centre is open to everyone without distinction. Membership is £1 a year and a clubroom and bar with background African music is reserved for members. On Friday evenings there is a discotheque until midnight and dancing to a band on Saturday evenings. The restaurant offers an attractive menu of African food at lunch-time and in the evening.

WHAT'S HAPPENING?

This chapter is concerned with entertainment, of the participating rather than the passive sort. It's not meant to be a guide to commercial entertainment, which is usually well advertised in the press and by posters in underground stations. It is rather a collection of opportunities for involvement, either at audience level or beyond. Many of the clubs listed have reciprocal membership arrangements with each other for the purchase of tickets, and the possession of an NUS (see p. 179) card usually entitles you to reduced admission.

GUIDES

TIME OUT (15p), the Living Guide to London, is easily the best guide to what's going on. It comes out weekly and contains up-to-the-minute news and events concerning theatre and film clubs, jazz/rock/folk groups, poetry readings, multi-media events, museum lectures, demonstrations and community projects. All editorial matter is free, so if you are on the inside of any project and want people to know about it, write to *Time Out* and they may give it a mention in the next issue. The copy date is always given on the front page and you send details to *Time Out*, 374 Gray's Inn Road, WC1.

WHAT'S ON IN LONDON (10p) comes out weekly on Fridays and is obtainable from most bookstalls. It's a comprehensive entertainments' guide which includes restaurants, cabarets and night life. Every month there is a shopping supplement.

THIS MONTH IN LONDON (15p) is a British Tourist Authority publication obtainable from most bookstalls.

WHAT'S ON FOR YOUNG PEOPLE (15p) comes out three

times a year in March, July and November. It's not just confined to London and gives details of museums, zoos, historic houses, sporting events, etc., over a wide area. Obtainable from most bookstalls.

OPEN AIR ENTERTAINMENT (10p) is published every summer season by the Greater London Council. It gives details of theatre, ballet and concert performances in London parks and includes a fold-up map of the parks and green spaces. Obtainable from most bookstalls.

MULTI-MEDIA PLACES

THE ROUNDHOUSE, Chalk Farm Road, NW1 [Box Office 485 – 8073].

The Roundhouse, by Chalk Farm underground station, was originally London's first turntable engine-shed, designed in 1846 by Robert Stephenson. It has been converted into a unique theatre equipped with some extraordinary acoustic and lighting devices. The stage and seating are liable to change from one show to another and there have been ice-shows and circuses as well as *Oh! Calcutta*. On Sundays there are usually pop shows, on weekdays theatre or films. There is a bar, coffee-bar and a restaurant which opens late at night and at lunchtime for non-members as well. There is a club membership which, for a small charge, keeps people in touch with what is going on.

THE INSTITUTE OF CONTEMPORARY ARTS, Nash House, The Mall, SW1 [930 – 0493], holds exhibitions of all kinds, lecture series, and multi-media events including poetry and music. These are open to the public but members get big reductions and there are special admission rates for NUS card holders. The coffee shop is open to the public and serves quite good and inexpensive food.

The £2 a year membership includes regular copies of the Eventsheet, advance bookings and reduced rates. The £5 a year membership includes as well invitations to opening parties and other social events. (See p. 101.)

THE COCKPIT, Gateforth Street, NW8 [262 – 7907] is the first

ILEA purpose-built youth arts workshop; and the first public London theatre-in-the-round to be built for 300 years. Events, times and prices of performances are advertised in *Time Out* and the *Guardian*, and you can book in advance. The theatre is available for hire by amateur and professional groups, and is free to those groups affiliated to the ILEA. Applications for theatre hire are considered in February, July and November for the following term.

As well as the theatre, there is a design and graphics workshop, a drama workshop, a youth theatre, a dance-drama group and a film-making group. There is also an electronic music lab with courses for beginners and composers, folk, jazz and poetry workshops, and the Centre's own contemporary music ensemble working in mixed media called 'Music Plus'. In the foyer are exhibitions of painting, sculpture and photography. Hanging space is free and groups or individuals should apply as for theatre hire.

The foyer coffee-bar is open for hot and cold snacks and a 'dish of the day' is served from 6.30 to 7.30 every evening and from 12.15 to 1.45 each lunchtime. There is also lunchtime entertainment.

OVAL HOUSE, Kennington Oval, SE11 [735 – 2786] offers a whole spectrum of creative opportunities for the 15–25 age group. There is socio-drama, jazz dance, dance drama, mime, street theatre, and some twelve defined drama groups, a regular evening jazz/rock workshop, a folk-music club, and a regular writers' workshop for poets and playwrights. There is a photographic lab, a small printing and graphics unit called 'Big Sister', and a film group.

All these activities are self-contained and self-programming under the Oval House umbrella, the members running the individual groups themselves.

Membership of the Club functions at two levels. Oval House full membership, open to people aged between 15 and 25, costs £2·10 a year and offers full access to the facilities and activities of the club. Oval House Theatre Club membership, open to people of all ages, costs 50p a year, and membership offers admission for audience participation, at reduced rates, to the regular programme of theatre, music, poetry, etc. Both memberships offer associate membership to other theatre and film clubs and vice versa. Oval House Group Membership is available to any Youth Theatre Group in Greater London.

The Club is open every evening from 7.30 to 11.30 p.m., all day Saturdays and all day Sundays.

DANCE

THE DANCE CENTRE, 12 Floral Street, Covent Garden, WC2 [836 – 6544] offers classes in classical ballet, tap, jazz, Spanish Flamenco, Caribbean movement, Afro-Cuban, etc., for both professionals and beginners. Their magazine *Move* (15p or 70p for a yearly subscription) lists their quarterly programme, but there are special events and short courses given by guest teachers as well. There is also a shop selling dancewear and an employment bureau for dancers who are resting.

THE DANCE BOOK CENTRE, 18 Hand Court, off High Holborn, WC1 [405 – 1414] sells books on all aspects of dance, and gramophone records for teaching purposes. They have a worldwide mail-order service.

THE PLACE, 17 Duke's Road, WC1 [387 – 0161] is the headquarters of the Contemporary Ballet Trust and the home of the London Contemporary Dance Theatre, a company of eighteen dancers directed by Robert Cohan, which performs works by major contemporary choreographers in regular London seasons. A converted drill hall includes a theatre, studios and licensed restaurant.

The Contemporary Ballet Trust also sponsors the London Contemporary Dance Group, a nucleus of three dancers and a speaker which provides a lecture-demonstration introducing Martha Graham's dance technique. The Group's programme is specially geared for colleges, schools and small theatres, combining education and entertainment. For organizations without much money to spare the programme can be presented by a lecturer and one dancer for a lower fee.

Also housed at The Place is the London School of Contemporary Dance which gives full- and part-time courses for professional training, introductory courses in Graham technique and intensive short courses during holiday periods. Special teenage classes and classes for children over six are held on Saturday mornings. Send for prospectus of details, including fees.

The London Contemporary Dance Workshop series is a link between the Company and the School which gives young choreographers, dancers, designers and musicians a chance of experimenting together and seeing their work performed in a professional atmosphere. The Workshop performances are free to members of the Artists' Place Society and have already produced four works of sufficiently high standard to be taken into the repertoire of the London Contemporary Dance Theatre. Full membership of the Artists' Place Society costs £5 a year and includes all the members of the one family, as well as restaurant facilities, attendance at classes, and a regular newsletter. This brings with it priority booking for first nights, and invitations to parties where you can meet the dancers of both the resident and visiting companies. The £2 a year ordinary membership entitles you to priority bookings and the newsletter, but not the social events. For temporary overseas visitors the ordinary membership is reduced to £1. Youth membership for under-sixteens is 50p. A lot of young people take out theatre membership for 50p a year for ticket purchase. There is reciprocal membership with the Young Vic, Oval House, The New Cinema Club and The Other Cinema. A £10 a year group membership for schools and societies offers big ticket reductions. For full details ring or write to the Membership Secretary.

Dance and Folk

CECIL SHARP HOUSE, 2 Regent's Park Road, NW1 [485 – 2206] is the home of the English Folk Dance and Song Society. Membership is £2·10 a year (£1·05 for students) but you don't have to be a member to go to any of the events or classes. There are classes in Country, Morris, Sword and Clog dancing as well as corn-dolly making.

On Saturday nights there is a Folk Dance upstairs and a Folk Cellar with singers and musicians downstairs. Every third Saturday, the singers and dancers get together for a ceilidh with specially invited guest artists.

During the week there are also classes in banjo, mandolin, and guitar and a fully equipped recording studio is available for hire.

There is also a Folk Shop where you can buy folk instruments, books and records, and the Vaughan Williams Memorial Library of books, records, tapes and photographs is open for use by anyone interested in folk song or music.

JAZZ, FOLK AND POP MUSIC

Regular folk and jazz sessions are held in pubs which you'll find listed, along with special musical events, in *Time Out* and the weekly *Melody Maker*. Gigs are held in various colleges and you need an NUS card to get in. There are occasional pop concerts in Hyde Park for everyone.

BUNJIE'S, 27 Litchfield Street, WC2 [240 – 1796] (by Leicester Square Station) is open every night with resident and guest folk-singers. Food and coffee available. Entrance 22½p.

THE MARQUEE, 90 Wardour Street, W1 [437 – 2375] opens seven nights a week with something different each night; jazz, folk, pop and usually progressive on Sundays. There is disco and dancing on Saturday nights. No membership is required and there is reduced admission for NUS card holders. Admission varies according to the night but is generally about 50p.

RONNIE SCOTT'S, 47 Frith Street, W1 [437 – 4239] is said to have the best jazz in London. Admission Monday to Thursday £1·50; Friday and Saturday £1·75. Membership is £1·05 a year but NUS card holders get free membership and reduced admission; 63p before 9.30 p.m. from Monday to Thursday.

UPSTAIRS AT RONNIE'S is a discotheque with a separate entrance.

THE LONDON YOUTH JAZZ ASSOCIATION is the parent body of the whole youth jazz movement. It was founded in 1965 by a group of teachers and musicians, disturbed at the lack of training facilities for young would-be jazz musicians and the lack of opportunity for them to meet and gain big band, reading and improvising experience.

There are annual week-long Easter jazz courses available to members, as well as regular free classes including big band and beginners' guitar. New classes can be started at any time if numbers justify it. These classes are held in the evenings at the Moberly Youth Centre, Kilburn Lane, W 10; the Sarah Siddons School, North Wharf Road, W 2; and Highbury Grove Youth Centre, Highbury Grove School, Highbury Grove, N 5.

Membership costs 50p per annum (all membership cards expire 31 August). The age range is, in theory, up to 21 but interested people in their early twenties can apply. Girls are particularly welcomed. Membership also includes free rehearsal facilities if required for a member's own jazz group. Many members have been found professional and semi-professional work through the Association and they can audition any time for either the London or the National Youth Jazz Orchestras.

For information and application form contact Bill Ashton, National Youth Jazz Association, 11 Victor Road, Harrow, Middlesex [863 – 2717].

See also jazz workshops *at the* COCKPIT *and* OVAL HOUSE, pp. 22–3.

CLASSICAL MUSIC

Promenade Concerts

Every summer a season of Promenade Concerts is given at the Royal Albert Hall, sponsored by the BBC. The season lasts for seven weeks and there is a concert every night, except for one or two Sundays. The repertoire is enormous, classical and modern composers being equally well represented. Tickets and programmes for the whole series are obtainable from the Royal Albert Hall and the usual agencies. A main feature of the concerts is the reasonable price of the tickets. If you are prepared to stand, a ticket for a single concert can cost as little as 30p and a season ticket costs £7·50. The concerts have a following of regulars, who get to know each other in the ticket queue and many keep in touch after the season is over.

After the last night of the proms there is an annual charity walk from Piccadilly to Stamford, Lincolnshire, to raise money for the Malcolm Sargent Cancer Fund for Children.

Clubs

THE LONDON SYMPHONY ORCHESTRA CLUB, 1 Montagu Street, WC1 [636 – 1704]. Membership of the Club entitles you to priority bookings for all London Symphony Orchestra concerts, passes for certain rehearsals, and you can also attend the regular meetings, talks, discussions and record recitals. The Club is closely linked with the LSO and its principal object is to further the interests of the orchestra by active participation and support. Annual subscription £1·50.

LONDON MUSICAL CLUB, 21 Holland Park, W11 [727 – 4440]. The Club is a centre where musicians and those who like to listen to music and talk about it may meet socially, or perform and practise. There are frequent concerts and recitals, and meetings and discussions are also arranged. A number of rooms are available for residents, and there is also a dining-room where members can have meals if they wish. Rehearsal rooms for groups and individual players are available for hire. Details of all charges can be obtained from the club. Annual subscription £2·10, students under 21, £1·05.

THE MUSIC CLUB OF LONDON, 36 Nottingham Place, W1 [486 – 4116]. The Club organizes a varied and extensive programme for people interested in music. Activities include interviews and talks by eminent musical personalities; series of talks on instruments of the orchestra, master classes, programmes on composers and other subjects of musical interest. Visits, tours and outings to places with special musical associations are arranged. The social side of the club includes wine-and-cheese parties and coffee evenings. Party bookings at reduced rates are arranged. Annual subscription £2 for the year you join, £1 thereafter.

Associations

THE NATIONAL FEDERATION OF MUSIC SOCIETIES, 29 Exhibition Road, SW7 [584 – 5797] publishes an annual handbook listing names and addresses of the secretaries of amateur choral and orchestral societies.

THE ERNEST READ MUSIC ASSOCIATION, 151 King Henry's Road, NW1 [722 – 9644].

The Association has a lot to offer those interested in music, whether performers or listeners. Best known for their seasons of concerts for children at the Royal Festival Hall, they also sponsor two amateur orchestras: the London Junior Orchestra and the London Senior Orchestra. Membership is by audition and you apply to the Association's headquarters. Instrumentalists pay an annual subscription of £3·15 for the Junior Orchestra, £4·20 for the Senior Orchestra. The Association has a choir which rehearses once a week during the autumn for an annual concert of Christmas music given in the Royal Albert Hall.

Every year two residential summer courses are held for orchestral players, one at Bradfield College and one at Roedean School. Although the courses are primarily for amateur musicians, nonplayers are welcome, both as listeners and helpers. Details from the Association.

LONDON ORCHESTRAL ASSOCIATION, 13–14 Archer Street, Shaftesbury Avenue, W1 [members 437 – 5027, office 437 – 1588]. This is an association of professional orchestral and dance musicians, with studios for teaching and ensemble practice. If you need private music lessons, the LOA can sometimes put you in touch with a teacher.

YOUTH AND MUSIC, 22 Blomfield Street, EC2 [588 – 4714]. Youth and Music was founded by Sir Robert Mayer in 1954 with the aim of drawing young people to music by giving them the opportunity to attend concerts, opera and ballet at greatly reduced prices. Individuals are not accepted as members. You join a local group, or form one of your own, and through the group apply for information about the concerts for which cheap tickets are available. Annual subscription is 25p and membership is restricted to those under 25. Full details can be had from the above address.

Singing

THE LONDON SYMPHONY ORCHESTRA CHORUS, 1 Montagu Street, WC1 [636 – 1704]. Admission to this famous amateur choir is by audition only, but you don't have a long wait for special audition days. Just write to the Honorary Secretary and ask for an audition. The Chorus rehearses regularly on Thursday evenings, with extra rehearsals when a concert is coming up. Concerts are given with the Orchestra. The Chorus organizes occasional social meetings such as a summer outing, but most of their time together is spent rehearsing.

THE CHANCERY SINGERS. Inquiries to Mr R. J. Tucker [242 – 2858, extension 12].

The Chancery Singers is a small choir of about thirty voices which rehearses every Monday and Thursday from 1.15 to 2.15 p.m. at Holy Trinity Church, Kingsway, WC2. Their tutor and conductor is Douglas Robinson, the chorus-master of the Royal Opera House, Covent Garden. The singers give frequent lunch-hour recitals with professional soloists and an orchestra from Covent Garden. Some previous singing experience is essential if you want to join the choir.

THE CHELSEA OPERA GROUP, Honorary Secretary, Dr R. C. Lock, 161 Coombe Lane, SW20 [947 – 0302].

This group of amateur players and singers performs three operas a year during university terms, usually once at Cambridge, once at Oxford and once in London. The group's orchestra is largely amateur but soloists and conductor are professional. Rehearsals begin six weeks before a performance, and are then called as often as is necessary. Membership is by audition only.

Floodlight (5p), the guide to evening classes published by the ILEA and on sale in most bookshops, gives details of madrigal choirs, male voice choirs, opera and light opera groups, as well as choral classes. Chamber music ensembles meet at various evening institutes, and individual tuition is available for some instruments. Enrolling usually begins in the second or third week of September. The City Literary Institute, Stukely Street, Drury Lane, WC2 [242 – 8558] is particularly strong on choral groups.

Poetry

THE POETRY SOCIETY, 21 Earls Court Square, SW5 [373 – 3556], 'provides a national service for poetry as a living art form'. It has poetry readings, discussion groups and a library of 15,000 books. Two weekend schools are organized per year at different universities. The Society publishes a quarterly journal, *Poetry Review*, and sponsors two annual poetry competitions, details of which can be got from the above address.

THE LONDON POETRY SECRETARIAT, Greater London Arts Association, Garrick House, 27 Southampton Street, WC2 [836 – 5225] is a joint venture of the GLAA and a founder group of poets called 'Poets in Public'. They act as an agency for performing poets who want to read their work. Organizers can contact them in order to be put in touch with suitable performers and the Secretariat has some money for grant allocation specially for this purpose.

There are many local poetry societies in London boroughs. Ask your public library for details.

Budding poets wanting to find a publisher should contact the Association of Little Presses, 148 King's Cross Road, WC1 [278 – 1966] who have a list.

See poetry workshops *at the* COCKPIT *and* OVAL HOUSE, pp. 22–3 *and see* Time Out.

NATIONAL BOOK LEAGUE, 7 Albemarle Street, W1 [493 – 9001] is a central meeting point for book people; there is a bar and a library for research. Annual membership, £4·20 for Londoners, £2·10 if you live over thirty miles outside. Initial entrance fee £1·05. Associate membership for students under 30, annual fee of £1·50 (£1·05 country) and no entrance fee.

THEATRE

THE NATIONAL YOUTH THEATRE, 81 Eccleston Square, SW1 [834 – 1085] aims at providing high standard theatre productions performed by young people for young people at prices they can afford. *Zigger Zagger, The Apprentices* and *Fuzz* were all plays written specially for them by Peter Terson. They now have a permanent theatre of their own, the Shaw Theatre, 100 Euston Road, by St Pancras Station which means they will be able to expand activities. More regular productions by the resident professional company; more holiday productions by NYT amateur companies; courses, demonstrations and lectures, as well as poetry readings, jazz sessions and pop concerts are planned for the future.

The National Youth Theatre is grant-aided. Membership is by audition and although they get hundreds of applications every year from all over the country every applicant is given an interview. The age range is from 14 to 21. No one should be put off through lack of experience or any feelings of inferiority or unsuitability.

THE YOUNG VIC, The Cut, Waterloo, SE1 [Inquiries to Old Vic Box Office 928 – 7616].

The Young Vic is an offshoot of the National Theatre Company whose home is at the Old Vic. Its aim is to provide classical and new plays of all types and every kind of theatrical experience for young people in their teens and early twenties, together with plays and entertainment for younger children and activities in which they can take part. Tickets for all seats in this new theatre, which holds 450 people, cost about 40p.

The Young Vic also invites other leading young theatre companies from England and abroad to play at the theatre. A mailing list keeps members informed about latest performances and activities for 40p yearly.

THE ENGLISH TEACHING THEATRE; tickets from International House (Room 1), 40 Shaftesbury Avenue, W1 [437 – 9167]. Every Tuesday at 7.30 there is a show which takes place in a theatre with professional actors and actresses, especially written for the foreign student. There are sketches, songs and dances, each of which has been written to demonstrate a point of grammar or pronunciation in English. So you watch a sketch, practise some of the sentences and then the audience sings a song along with the actors. As the organizers say, it's far more fun than a language laboratory, and you can, of course, take a friend along too.

THE GREATER LONDON ARTS ASSOCIATION, Garrick House, 27 Southampton Street, WC2 publishes a list (17½p) of the seventy or so 'little theatres' in London, which are available for hire by amateur companies. *(See p. 111.)*

Courses

THE BRITISH DRAMA LEAGUE, 9 Fitzroy Square, W1P 6AE [387 – 2666].

Their library is the largest collection of plays and theatre books in the country. Service to members by post or personal call. They also have an information service for individual and affiliated groups. Regular visits to West End productions are arranged through their Theatregoers' Club.

They run one-day and weekend courses on theatre design and costume, stage management and production and acting, as well as summer schools and Junior Drama League holiday courses. Apply to the Organizer of the Training Department.

THE CURTAIN THEATRE (late Toynbee Theatre), 26 Commercial Street, E1 [247 – 6788] is a School of Stagecraft for ILEA affiliated groups and a performance area for professional and educational theatre. Short courses are held for 14-year-olds upwards as well as for teachers and a resident team welcomes requests for assistance with projects. For details of courses available, apply to the Manager.

THEATRE CENTRE LTD, Victor Road, NW10 [969 – 7959]. Theatre Centre companies visit schools and clubs in theatreless areas. A large range of lectures and courses is available for teachers and youth leaders. For full details, including fees, write to the Administrator.

Theatre Clubs which run courses

THE QUESTORS THEATRE, Mattock Lane, Ealing, W5 [567 –
0011] offers a unique two-year part-time course for serious
amateurs which takes place two evenings a week and on Saturdays
so that it can be combined with a job. This student training course
is aimed primarily but not exclusively at training actors and
actresses for the main acting group of the Questors Theatre and
is run in conjunction with the London Borough of Ealing Education Committee. Anyone over 17 may apply (there is no upper
age limit) and will be given an interview and audition. The first-
year course costs £4·50. Application form and details from the
Administrator.

The Questors Theatre also runs eight regular weekly groups
providing an opportunity for young people between the ages of
5 and 19 to participate in theatre activity.

The Questors is an amateur Theatre Club founded in 1929, and
now acknowledged as one of the leading 'little theatres' in this
country. Acting members are auditioned but there are plenty of
jobs backstage and audience members are welcome. Membership
costs £2·50 per year; full-time students and under 18s, £1 per
year. Members see at least ten productions each year without
further charge.

Other activities of the Club include film shows, exhibitions of
painting and poetry readings.

MOUNTVIEW THEATRE CLUB, 104 Crouch Hill, N8 [340 –
5885] is another well-known 'little theatre' club. It stages twenty-
five plays annually; although a large company they audition for
experienced actors. Would-be directors and designers should
bring photographs of their work when they come for an interview.
Full membership for those participating in the work of the theatre
is £3·20 a year and associate membership for the purpose of
purchasing tickets and membership of the club bar is 65p a year.
Apply to the Secretary for details.

Mountview Theatre School offers a variety of courses, daytime
and evening, full-time and part-time, acting and technical. These
courses are subsidized by Haringey Education Committee and
many other education authorities throughout the country. It also

runs a special course for coloured actors with emphasis on voice production and many opportunities for regular stage production. Many of the students on this course come from abroad and return to their own countries to work in theatre there. The school produces thirty-five or more plays each year. For prospectus of day or evening school, apply to the Registrar.

Other Theatre Clubs

HAMPSTEAD THEATRE CLUB, The Civic Centre, Swiss Cottage, NW3 [Box Office 722 – 9301, administration 722 – 9074]. Full membership is £1 a year. Honorary membership is available to anyone holding a Camden library card and is free of charge. You don't however get the monthly members' newsletter and can't book for first nights or Saturday night performances. There is also a student membership for 50p a year with reduced seat prices.

STAGE TWO, 109a Regent's Park Road, Chalk Farm, NW1 [586 – 4164] is an interesting new extension to the Hampstead Theatre Club: an experimental workshop where the small group of permanent actors and actresses both create and perform their own work in collaboration with composers, sculptors and musicians.

TOWER THEATRE, Canonbury Tower, Canonbury Place, N1 [226 – 5111] is the home of the Tavistock Repertory Company who put on three seasons of classical and contemporary plays a year. Membership of the theatre club, £1·25 a year, entitles you to attend talks, play readings and social events which are held in the Tudor panelled rooms of Canonbury Tower, which remains much as it looked in the sixteenth century. But as the theatre is licensed to the public, membership is not required to see a play. People interested in acting membership should contact the Auditions Secretary. Anyone can be put on the mailing list for 15p a year. The Box Office is open from 10 a.m. to 6 p.m. at the Canonbury Bookshop, 268 Upper Street, N1 [226 – 3475] or at the theatre from 7 to 9 p.m.

UNITY THEATRE, 1 Goldington Street, NW1 [387 – 8647]. Unity began as the theatre of protest in the thirties, the theatre which first brought the works of Brecht to the English stage. It is still politically committed and puts on many new plays, political revues and satire. The theatre is managed by a committee elected by the membership. Members pay £1 a year which entitles them to take part in activities, to vote and to stand for election on to the Committee. Auditions are held every six weeks. There is an associate membership for the purchase of tickets.

Transpontine Theatre

THE GREENWICH THEATRE (Director: Ewan Hooper), Crooms Hill, SE10 [Box Office 858 – 7755].

The new Greenwich Theatre is a marvellous example of what can be done with the support and enthusiasm of local residents who feel the need for a living theatre. The old Hippodrome was in its time an old music hall, then a cinema, and finally ended its days as a derelict warehouse. It was due for demolition when it was rescued by the Greenwich Theatre Trust and renovated. Inside the theatre is an art gallery, a restaurant which is also open at lunchtime, a bar, and a coffee-bar. One of the pleasantest ways of getting to the theatre for a matinée or a Saturday performance is by river; by boat from Westminster, Charing Cross or Tower Piers. There are also regular trains from Charing Cross main line station to Greenwich.

THE YOUNG PEOPLE'S THEATRE (Director: Roger Sell), 13 Nevada Street, SE10 [858 – 4447], which is attached to the Greenwich Theatre, includes the Bowsprit Company and the Youth Theatre. The Bowsprit visits local schools and forms a valuable link with the community. The Youth Theatre provides drama/arts work for anyone over 7 years of age, talented or otherwise. All young people are welcome. They have their own premises in a deconsecrated church in Burrage Road, Plumstead, which they are gradually converting into a Youth and Community Arts Centre.

SOUTH LONDON THEATRE CENTRE, 2a Norwood High Street, West Norwood, SE27 [670 – 3474, any evening after 7.30 p.m.]. This is a community project housed in an old fire station which the members themselves converted. This amateur repertory company presents ten plays a season, one a month which runs for seven nights. There is plenty of scope for a variety of skills: carpentry, sewing, typing and photography. There are classes in stage design and lighting, as well as acting courses and a dance drama class on Saturdays. The Centre is open every evening including Sundays, from 7.30 to 11 p.m. Each month they hang paintings, the work of the South East London Arts Group, in the bar lounge. Full annual membership is £3, but membership of 50p a year enables you to buy tickets. Inquiries to the Membership Officer.

Young Theatre Groups

GROUP 64, YOUTH THEATRE WORKSHOP, 203 Upper Richmond Road, Putney, SW15 [228 – 8437, evenings].

Group 64 meets in a converted church. There are no auditions for membership and people willing to slosh paint, joiners, designers, etc. are wanted just as much as those who want to act. They do one play a month. There is a Sunday-night folk club as well as other activities related to the arts. The age range is 15–25.

HEATHAM HOUSE, Whitton Road, Twickenham [892 – 5063] is a Youth Activities Centre for the 14s to 21s which has a varied programme, including a theatre group which meets on Wednesday evenings.

HOLLAND PARK LINK DRAMA GROUP. Organizer P. R. Fozzard, 36a Fitzgeorge Avenue, W14 [603 – 6738].

Despite the title, membership isn't confined to former members of Holland Park School. There is no subscription and no rigid organization. The group works principally to present plays. There is a regular business meeting on Sunday nights but other meetings depend on work in progress. For the place of meeting, contact the Organizer. The age range is 16–25.

MINERVA YOUTH THEATRE. Correspondence to 21 Lindale, Wimbledon Park Road, SW19.

This group has no permanent home as yet. Meantime they meet at the Harrow Club, Latimer Road on Wednesdays and use the theatre at the Christopher Wren School, Bloemfontein Road, Shepherds Bush, W11 on Mondays and Fridays. They don't audition for actors. In fact they don't want people to come along just for the acting but to take part in everything, making scenery, props, etc. The age range is 16–25.

TUFNELL THEATRE, Acland Burghley School, Burghley Road, NW5 [485 – 8993].

Two groups meet here, Tufnell Theatre and Teenage Theatre, on Tuesdays and Fridays, 7.30–9.30 p.m. The age range is 17–24.

Puppet Theatre

THE LITTLE ANGEL MARIONETTE THEATRE, 14 Dagmar Passage, N1 [226 – 1787] is the only permanent puppet theatre in England. It seats 100 and holds shows every weekend including Sundays. For 25p you can be on their mailing list and get news of forthcoming shows.

THE EDUCATIONAL PUPPETRY ASSOCIATION, 23a Southampton Place, WC1 meets every Monday evening during termtime from 6.30 p.m. onwards and students or anyone wanting to know more about puppetry are welcome to drop in. They also run occasional vacation courses. There is a magazine, newsletter and library service for members. Send a stamped, addressed envelope for details.

Classes in puppetry are advertised in *Floodlight*.

FILMS

For tracking down the whereabouts of current commercial feature films going the rounds, phone the following information desks: RANK [828 – 0126] and ABC [437 – 9234].

Interesting foreign and British films are shown at the following cinemas:

ACADEMY CINEMAS, 165–7 Oxford Street, W1. [Academy One, 437 – 2981; Academy Two, 437 – 5129; Academy Three, 437 – 8819]; EVERYMAN, Holly Bush Vale, Hampstead, NW3 [435 – 1525]; and PARIS PULLMAN, Drayton Gardens, SW10 [373 – 5898] which shows late-night films as well.

Late-night films are also shown at several Classic and Odeon cinemas. It's a good way to catch up on an old film you missed at the time, but these films are shown subject to demand for two to three days at a time and are liable to be taken off at short notice.

If you live in an area with Indian and Pakistani shops, you'll see advertisements for Indian films, which are usually shown on a Sunday afternoon at a local cinema. You may have to join the appropriate film society to get in, unless you can go as someone's guest. Most of these films aren't subtitled, which is a pity because the plots are Shakespearean in complexity, but there is always lots of song and dance and it's often worth going just for the scenery and the background music.

Film Clubs

Membership of a film club is one way of seeing interesting and important films from all over the world which don't normally get a wide commercial showing.

THE NATIONAL FILM THEATRE, South Bank, Waterloo, SE1 [928 – 3232] and THE BRITISH FILM INSTITUTE, 81 Dean Street, London W1 [437 – 4355].

The National Film Theatre is run as a club for members and associates of the British Film Institute. Associate membership of £1 per year (75p for students) enables you to purchase tickets. It shows around 400 films a year from all over the world including early silent films, rare film comedies and great film classics.

Full membership (£2.25) of the British Film Institute offers, as well as ticket purchase, the use of the Book and Stills Library, the film hire service at a 25 per cent discount, and use of the information department. Also included is a free subscription to *Sight and Sound*. Both members and associates are on the mailing list for forthcoming programmes and get free admission to celebrity lectures and other occasional special shows.

There is a licensed club with light refreshments available to members, associates, and their guests. Open daily 5.30–11 p.m., Sundays 7–10 p.m.

THE BRITISH FEDERATION OF FILM SOCIETIES is in the same building as the British Film Institute, with the same telephone number. They have a booklet listing affiliated film societies in this country and abroad, with a section on film societies in London.

THE NEW CINEMA CLUB, 122 Wardour Street, W1 [734 – 5888] will send you a free copy of its forthcoming programme for the next few months. Full membership is £1·25 a year, student membership 50p and visitors' membership 25p a month. This also entitles you to buy tickets for many other film clubs including the Roundhouse, Institute of Contemporary Arts, and the Electric Cinema.

THE ELECTRIC CINEMA CLUB, 191 Portobello Road, W11 [727 – 4992]. Membership 10p a year, admission 30p. They recognize membership of a large number of other cinema clubs.

THE OTHER CINEMA, 12–13 Little Newport Street, WC2 [734 8508]. Membership 25p. Ring for details.

COUNTERACT (formerly ANGRY ARTS). Inquiries to 6 Bramshill Gardens, NW5 [263 – 0613].

Counteract put on films with social and political implications. They believe however that there is a limited value in just showing a film alone; that a film has an important part to play in a related wider environmental context, and so, after showing a film, they initiate discussion amongst the audience. This can take the form of small group discussions or even improvised drama and they have used street plays from time to time. Membership is 25p per year. You can join on the night and members can bring up to three friends. See *Time Out* for programmes.

See also film workshops *at the* COCKPIT *and* OVAL HOUSE, pp. 22–3, *and see* Floodlight *for film-making classes.*

ARTS AND CRAFTS

THE CRAFTS CENTRE OF GREAT BRITAIN, 43 Earlham Street, Covent Garden, WC2 [240 – 3327] exhibits and sells work by Britain's best artists and craftsmen. The work displayed is modern rather than folksy, changes frequently and can include furniture, pottery, rugs, jewellery and sculpture. Once knitting was featured as an art form in an original display of wall-hangings and lampshades, constructed by using broom handles as knitting needles.

THE GLASSHOUSE, 27 Neal Street, Covent Garden, WC2 [836 – 9785] (next door to the Crafts Centre) is Britain's first glass studio workshop. Artists can hire the small furnaces by the day to blow their own glass and the public can come in and watch. The Glasshouse is open from 10 a.m. to 5 p.m. Monday to Friday. The artists' work is on show around the studio and is all for sale, wholesale and retail. A three-week course consisting of three evenings a week is available at approximately £20 which includes all materials, tools, etc. Further details from the Studio Manager.

CAMDEN ARTS CENTRE, 54 Arkwright Road, NW3 [435 – 2643 and 5224] is open six days a week, closes on Mondays, and there are three sessions each day: mornings 10 a.m.–1 p.m.; afternoons 2–5 p.m.; and evenings 7–9 p.m. Classes include painting, pottery and silk screen printing and cost anything from £5 to £12 a year, which includes materials. There is also an exhibition gallery open from 11 a.m. to 8 p.m. Tuesday to Saturday, and on Sundays from 2 to 7 p.m.

THE CHELSEA POTTERY, 13 Radnor Walk, SW3 [352 – 1366] is an open studio for beginners, experienced amateurs and wheelless professionals. It costs £7·35 a year to join and facilities are available between 9 a.m. and 9 p.m. each weekday. Individual lessons are £1 an hour and there are joint sessions for 50p on Saturday mornings and afternoons, especially for children.

HAMPSTEAD POTTERY AND ARTS CENTRE, 4 Perrins Lane, NW3 [435 – 9589]. Work produced at this pottery is on show and on sale here and there are also regular exhibitions by wellknown potters. Classes are held in the evenings.

SUSAN MEYER-MICHAEL, 99 North End Road, NW11 [455 – 0817] is a potter who enjoys teaching children and adults. Her studio is at her home and the charge is £1.07½ per two-hour session including clay and tools. Firing is extra. There are two Saturday sessions, 10 a.m.–12 noon, and 2–4 p.m., and sessions on other days by arrangement.

YOURE SHOP LTD, 26–8 Camden Passage, N1 [359 – 1204] will accept good quality home-made articles on a sale or return basis. They add 60 per cent on to the price as their commission. On sale in the shop are belts, sandals, dresses, toys, cushions, candles, etc., and it's an interesting place to buy original and inexpensive things. The idea of Youre Shop proved so successful that they have opened another, YOURE OTHER SHOP, 17 South End Green,

NW3 [794 – 7053] which sells mainly pottery, posters and jewellery.

There is a very wide range of classes in *Floodlight* and also the leaflet on day classes obtainable from County Hall, SE1. Their Education Inquiries Department will give advice and further information about classes. Call, or phone 633 – 5000.

MARKETS

Indoor Markets

KENSINGTON MARKET, 49 Kensington High Street, W8. A mixture of stalls selling antiques, clothes, both secondhand and new, posters, etc., on three floors. Stalls are available to rent.

Opposite Kensington Market, on the other side of the road is THE ANTIQUE HYPERMARKET, 26–40 Kensington High Street, W8 where all the 100 or so dealers guarantee to refund the money on any item unwittingly sold which turns out to be fake.

ANTIQUE SUPERMARKET, 5 Barrett Street, W1 (between Oxford Street and Wigmore Street). Mondays to Saturdays, 10 a.m.–6 p.m.

CHELSEA ANTIQUE MARKET, 252 King's Road, SW3. Monday, 10 a.m.–1 p.m.; Tuesday to Saturday, 10 a.m.–6 p.m.

Street Markets

Monday to Saturday

BERWICK STREET MARKET, Soho, W1. Fruit, vegetables, clothes, cloth.

BRIXTON MARKET, off Brixton Road, SW2 spreads over several streets including Electric Avenue. Fruit, vegetables and secondhand clothes. Fewer stalls on Mondays and Wednesdays.

CHAPEL MARKET, White Conduit Street, N1 (near Liverpool Road). Fruit, vegetables, secondhand clothes. Closed Thursday and Saturday afternoons.

SHEPHERDS BUSH MARKET, W12, situated between Goldhawk Road and Shepherds Bush Metropolitan underground station. A wide variety of stalls. Closed Thursday afternoons.

Lunch-time, Monday to Friday

LEATHER LANE, Holborn, EC1. A variety of stalls including clothes.

Fridays: dawn till 4.30 p.m.

CALEDONIAN MARKET, Bermondsey Street, SE1 (near London Bridge station). Antiques and lots of junk stalls.

Saturdays

CAMDEN PASSAGE, Upper Street, Islington, N1 (near Angel underground station). Stalls selling antiques and junk.

PORTOBELLO ROAD, W11 (near Notting Hill Gate underground station). Antiques, junk and tat.

In both markets there are galleries with stalls which are available for renting.

Sundays

PETTICOAT LANE, Middlesex Street, E1 (near Liverpool Street station). A variety of stalls selling crockery, clothes, etc. 9 a.m.–2 p.m.

SCLATER STREET, off Bethnal Green Road, E1. Animals, birds, reptiles. 8.30 a.m.–1 p.m.

Wholesale Markets

COVENT GARDEN (Covent Garden underground station). Fruit, vegetables and the Floral Hall. Open 5.30 a.m. Floral Hall open till around 10.30 a.m.

BILLINGSGATE FISH MARKET, Lower Thames Street, EC3. The oldest market in London. Open from 5.30 a.m.

SMITHFIELD, Charterhouse Street, EC1 (nearest underground station, Farringdon). Meat. The largest meat market in the world. Opens at 6 a.m.

AUDIENCE SHOWS

Tickets for radio and TV audience shows can be obtained free from the following addresses. It's as well not to be too specific in asking for a particular show because there are waiting lists and your show may have finished its run by the time your name comes up. But if you state a preference for the type of programme you'd like to see, i.e. pop show, quiz, comedy, etc. it helps, and mentioning your age group gives them a clue. Write rather than ring.

TICKET UNIT, BBC, London W1A AA for radio and TV shows. The TV shows take place fairly centrally, mostly at the BBC Television Centre, Wood Lane, Shepherds Bush, W12.

TICKET OFFICE, THAMES TELEVISION, Television House, 306 Euston Road, NW1. They record mainly at Elstree and Teddington studios.

TICKET OFFICE, LONDON WEEKEND TV, Station House, Harrow Road, Wembley, Middlesex. Over-15s only.

HOW IT'S DONE

Television Tour

ITA TELEVISION GALLERY, 70 Brompton Road, SW3 [584 – 7011] tells the story of television, past and present. You can see the early experiments, as well as how programmes are created, produced and transmitted. The tour takes one and a half hours. Starting times are 10 a.m., 11.30 a.m., 2.30 p.m. and 4 p.m., Mondays to Fridays. Admission is free. Write or ring for a booking. Over 16s only.

Newspaper Tours

DAILY MAIL: Production Manager, Associated Newspapers Ltd, New Carmelite House, Carmelite Street, EC4. Tours from Monday to Friday, 9–11.15 p.m. Over-14s only. Write well in advance, at least three months.

EVENING STANDARD: Works Manager, Evening Standard, 47 Shoe Lane, EC4. Tours on weekday afternoons beginning at 2 p.m. and lasting two hours. Parties of fifteen people. Write well in advance.

NEWS OF THE WORLD: Production Manager, 30 Bouverie Street, EC4 [353 – 3030]. Saturday evenings only. Groups of twelve people; they fit in twelve groups during the evening. The first tour begins at 7 p.m., the last is at 10.30 p.m. Tour lasts one hour. People can usually be fitted in at short notice.

SUN: Tours from Mondays to Fridays at 8.30 p.m. and 10.30 p.m. Apply as for *News of the World*.

DAILY TELEGRAPH: 135 Fleet Street, EC4 [353 – 4242]. Tours from Mondays to Fridays at 8.45 p.m. lasting two hours. Parties of eight to ten people. Ring up or write well in advance as there's a waiting list of around eight months.

THE TIMES: [236 – 2000]. Tours from Mondays to Fridays from 8.30 p.m. to 10.30 p.m. Parties of sixteen people. Ring six months in advance. Minimum age 16.

3

BELONGING AND DOING

The British have a reputation for forming voluntary societies to get things done. Those listed here fall into five main categories: service to the local community; protection of the environment; service to the international community; pressure and political groups; and religious organizations. There are in addition further organizations which for one reason or another have been listed in other sections of the book, but which we cross-refer you to in the index below. There is one factor which all the organizations named here have in common: that you don't just join them, you can also participate in their work.

Service to the Local Community

Protection of the Environment

Service to the International Community

Pressure Groups and Politics

Religious Organizations

SERVICE TO THE LOCAL COMMUNITY

BLOOD DONORS. Blood transfusion has become an essential part of modern surgery. The number of patients given transfusions and the amount of blood used rises steadily and to keep pace with this two donors are needed for every minute of every hour, day and night. Thinking about donating blood for the first time makes many people understandably nervous. There is really no need to be, and once you have had the courage to begin, you will wonder why you ever hesitated.

By telephoning any of the following numbers, you can get any information a potential donor may require, including the time and place of your nearest blood-donor clinic.

North London Blood Transfusion Centre, Deansbrook Road, Edgware, Middlesex [952 – 5511].

N.E. Metropolitan Regional Blood Transfusion Centre, Crescent Drive, Brentwood, Essex [Brentwood 3545].

South London Blood Transfusion Centre, 38 Stanley Road, Sutton, Surrey [642 – 8221].

BRITISH ASSOCIATION OF SETTLEMENTS, 10 St George's House, Toynbee Hall, 28 Commercial Street, E1 [247 – 8689].

A settlement is a residential or non-residential community centre engaged in the encouragement and extension of educational, cultural, recreational and community services in the neighbourhood. The settlements have grown from their Victorian beginnings in 1884 and an accent is now laid on community action – the initiation of social change through local leadership.

Settlements need both residential and non-residential volunteers to help with such activities as holiday play-schemes, family welfare counselling, youth-club work, visiting and running clubs for the old and the handicapped, prison after-care work, and also with the clerical and organizational work of the settlement. Residential staff may have full-time jobs elsewhere or may be students who wish to gain practical social-work experience. The residents live simply and pay £6–7 per week for board and lodging. The amount of time given to the settlement varies according to circumstances and personal capacities.

There are nineteen settlements in the Greater London area. A list of addresses is available from the Association.

The following example shows the sort of work which may be going on in any one settlement at any given time.

The Blackfriars Settlement, 44–7 Nelson Square, SE1 [928 – 9521] is a centre for community care. It needs regular help from volunteers in its various activities in the neighbourhood. These include work with families, youth work, Young Mums' clubs, where children are cared for in the nursery while mothers can meet, discuss and relax, a holiday centre at Deal for family and children's holidays, clubs for the blind and for the elderly, and an occupational work centre for the physically and mentally handicapped. During the summer holidays, the Settlement runs two schemes for children. One takes children daily for a fortnight to Greenwich Park, the other, which runs for three weeks, is a combination of activities in the morning (carpentry, painting, dancing, etc.) based at the Youth Centre and small group visits (swimming, museums, etc.) in the afternoon.

BRITISH COUNCIL OF CHURCHES YOUTH DEPARTMENT, 10 Eaton Gate, SW1 [730 – 9611].

The ecumenical movement is concerned not only with inter-denominational relations, but also with relations between church and society as a whole. The Youth Department organizes social-service work camps, exchange programmes and international visits and conferences. Work camps are usually for people aged between 18 and 30 and are run in places as far apart as Smethwick in the midlands and Lutendele in the Congo. Volunteers pay fares and contribute to living expenses. Continuing involvement is possible through a local group, which may be running an open youth club, giving community service, studying together, or may exist for a short period only, to concern itself with a particular facet of ecumenism.

BRITISH RED CROSS SOCIETY, County of London Branch, 34 Grosvenor Gardens, SW1 [730 – 0677].

The aim of the Society is to help the victims of war, natural disaster or accident, the sick, aged and handicapped. Volunteers can give a wide variety of help in hospitals, clinics and first-aid posts (running canteens and trolley shops, interpreting, and visiting the lonely and chronic sick), in people's homes (reading to the blind, teaching handicrafts), in clubs for the handicapped, in residential homes, and on holidays for the old or the disabled, with youth leadership in the Junior Red Cross. The Red Cross arranges certified training courses in first-aid, nursing, maternal and child welfare, social welfare, hygiene and public health.

CAMBRIDGE HOUSE LITERACY SCHEME, 131 Camberwell Road, SE5 [703 – 5025].

There are many people who for one reason or another reach adulthood unable to read or write. Through the scheme they are given individual home tuition, one and a half hours per week, by volunteers. All applicants are considered as volunteers, but those with teaching experience of some kind are naturally most sought after. Training courses are held every six months and there are also occasional refresher conferences.

CASUALTIES UNION, 1 Grosvenor Crescent, SW1 [235 – 5366].

First-aid trainers need simulated casualties as a training aid. The Casualties Union provides them. Volunteer members pay an annual subscription of 75p and join a study circle for a series of weekly or fortnightly classes over a period of about nine months. At the study circle you learn how to make up realistic wounds and act the part of a casualty, and how to simulate such things as broken limbs, epileptic fits, mental illness, hysteria and strokes. Study circles have a minimum of six and a maximum of twenty people and work on a self-instruction scheme with medical supervision. After completing the course there is a 'proficiency' test before medical judges. Then the volunteer is ready for requests from first-aid trainers for 'a mutilated body which will groan and bleed authentically', 'a ward-full of mentally ill patients' or 'a coach-load of accident victims'.

CHILDREN'S COUNTRY HOLIDAY FUND, 1 York Street, Baker Street, W1 [935 – 8353].

The CCHF has for many years assisted in providing holidays in the country and at the seaside for children in need. Voluntary help is needed in the organization of these holidays, such as interviewing parents, escorting children and supervising at camps.

THE CHILDREN'S SOCIETY MEMO CLUB, 19 Hanover Square, W1 [499 – 0600].

Memo Club is open to anyone who works in an office, from the typists' pool to the chairman's suite, and to commercial students. The Club's one object is to enable members to become partners in the work the Children's Society is doing for deprived children. You join by paying a once-and-for-all enrolment fee of 25p. You will then be sent a membership card and a list of fund-raising ideas. All members are asked to raise funds for the Society, and in addition you can help children in one of the Society's ninety-five Children's Homes by taking a personal interest in their welfare.

COMMUNITY SERVICE VOLUNTEERS, 23 Commercial Street, E1 [247 – 8113].

CSV organizes medium-term service projects in this country.

To volunteer you must be at least 17 and determined to serve other people. No other qualification is necessary. The minimum period of service is four months but, the longer you serve, the more responsibility you can be given. As a volunteer you will live away from home and get board and lodging, and pocket money of about £2 a week.

CSV tries to find a project as near as possible to what you want to do. Volunteers have helped young immigrants to learn English, worked in approved schools, hospitals, adventure playgrounds, housing associations for the homeless; they have worked with alcoholics, with the disabled, and on projects to improve the natural environment. They work wherever there is an area of human need.

CSV also runs an advisory service which suggests suitable work for any group at any time. It publishes specialist papers on such things as running a children's holiday scheme, home decorating, fund raising, etc.

CONSUMER GROUPS, National Federation of Consumer Groups, 14 Buckingham Street, WC2 [930 – 0258].

A Consumer Group is concerned with promoting the interests of consumers and improving the standard of goods and services in its area. The groups are autonomous, but the National Federation coordinates their efforts and provides a national voice for their activities. It will supply information on existing local groups and advice on how to start one. The groups concentrate on fact-finding, publicizing the information gathered and, where appropriate, taking action upon it. Some of the matters with which groups have concerned themselves are the comparative prices and availability of goods, hygiene in shops, restaurants and public lavatories, and the cost of such services as television rental, garage services and restaurant facilities, the effectiveness of public services such as libraries, hospitals and refuse collection. The Islington Consumer Group organized a successful campaign to retain the municipal bath service. Members pay an annual subscription of from 50p to £1 per household and this entitles them to the Group's quarterly news sheet. The degree of involvement in local activities is a matter of individual choice.

CONTACT, 41a Monserrat Road, SW15 [486 – 4808].

Contact's aim is to encourage volunteers to give one Sunday afternoon a month to take old people out by car to private homes in or near London where they meet people from their own area and are entertained to tea. Contact needs volunteers (with or without cars) and hosts in and around London who can entertain up to twenty-four people to tea.

DUKE OF EDINBURGH'S AWARD SCHEME, 2 Old Queen Street, SW1 [930 – 7681].

This scheme is open to anyone between the ages of 14 and 21. Through participation in one or all of three Awards, it encourages the learning of new hobbies and skills, the training for and giving of voluntary service and the organization of expeditions of varying distances. There are also physical activity and 'Design for Living' projects. The Scheme is not a competition. It is an award for personal effort and persistence rather than brains or brawn. It is not an organization. No one belongs as a member and you may take part as an individual or through your firm, club, school or other organization. To take part you must first get a record-book from your local youth office, school, club or firm and then choose activities from each of the four sections.

GREATER LONDON ASSOCIATION FOR THE DISABLED, 183 Queensway, W2 [727 – 4426].

The Association runs clubs for disabled adults, advises on holidays and arranges home-visiting. In all these activities it depends to a large extent on volunteers who can offer one evening a fortnight for club work, or who can do regular home-visiting at any time during the day.

GREATER LONDON CONFERENCE ON OLD PEOPLE'S WELFARE, 99 Great Russell Street, WC1 [636 – 4864].

The Conference brings together interested organizations in London to discuss the needs of old people, provides an information and advisory service for local old people's welfare committees and promotes recreational activities and experimental services for old people.

Voluntary workers are usually needed during the day in old people's clubs. Entertainers, choir leaders and accompanists are also required.

INTERNATIONAL VOLUNTARY SERVICE, 91 High Street Harlesden, NW10 [965 – 1446].

IVS is an international membership-based organization with over 100 local units in Britain. These units do continuing work in their areas with the old, the young, the under-privileged and the lonely. IVS runs international work camps in Britain and Europe, medium-term service projects (six months upwards) in Britain and Europe, and long-term service projects for qualified volunteers in the developing countries. They also recruit volunteers after a national emergency, such as the floods in Florence or the Sicilian earthquakes. You can work with a local unit at any age, go to a British work camp at 16, go to a foreign work camp and volunteer for medium-term service at 18, and to work overseas you must be 21.

JEWISH YOUTH VOLUNTARY SERVICE, 33 Henriques Street, E1 [709 – 1654].

Voluntary service projects are organized both within and beyond the Jewish community.

LEND A HAND, 20 Cambridge Park, E11 [989 – 9044].

Lend a Hand is a twenty-four hour distress unit covering all facets of social work. Anybody can seek help on any problem from a housing difficulty to a personal or health problem. Help is given by voluntary workers on a part-time basis and volunteers from the age of 16 upwards are always urgently needed.

LONDON COUNCIL OF SOCIAL SERVICE, 68 Chalton Street, NW1 [388 – 0241].

The Council is a coordinating body for social-work organizations and activities throughout the Greater London area. The Council will put you in touch with your local Council of Social Service or an organization in your area which would be glad of the kind of help you want to offer. The Council publishes *Opportunities for Voluntary Social Service in London* (17½p) which lists nearly 200 organizations needing volunteer help.

LONDON MARRIAGE GUIDANCE COUNCIL, 76a New Cavendish Street, W1 [580 – 1087].

The Council is concerned with marriage counselling, helping people in the preparation for marriage and with the emotional relationships and problems of young people. Volunteer counsellors, between the ages of 25 and 50, are needed to help with this work. Careful selection, basic training and continuing in-service training and support are provided. Counsellors should be able to give about six hours weekly between 10 a.m. and 9 p.m. on a regular basis.

NACRO, 125 Kennington Park Road, SE11 [735 – 1151].

NACRO, the National Association for the Care and Resettlement of Offenders, is the voluntary organization concerned with crime prevention and the after-care of offenders. Its members are voluntary organizations, professional workers, and individuals who work to prevent ex-offenders from relapsing into further crime, through help and support both to them and their families. In London NACRO organizes the following facilities for prisoners and their families:

NACRO Voluntary Associates (Inner London), which is sponsored jointly by NACRO and the Inner London Probation and After Care Service, encourages the involvement of volunteers in work with offenders and their families. Regular courses are run for those who wish to be involved in this work, consisting of weekly lectures and discussion groups extending over a period of about eight weeks. (Details from the Organizer, 25 Camberwell Grove, SE5.) At the end of the course, volunteers apply for selection to be accredited for this work. Volunteer associates then work in groups with a probation officer. The work might be casework with ex-prisoners, especially those who are homeless; giving support and practical help to young offenders; giving on-going support to prisoners' wives and their families.

NACRO Lodgings Scheme helps homeless prisoners to find understanding lodgings.

NACRO Homeless Families Advice Centre is linked with Shelter to help offenders' families threatened with eviction or living in slum conditions.

PHAB, National Association of Youth Clubs, 30 Devonshire Street, W1 [935 – 2941].

PHAB stands for Physically Handicapped and Able Bodied young people who come together for regular meetings and residential training courses. There are about twenty courses a year designed to give people the opportunity to share and learn more about common interests. The mornings are spent working at a chosen interest such as art, music, drama, field studies or film making, and the afternoon and evening programmes include outdoor activities, visits and entertainments. The course fees are £12 but some grant aid may be given by local education authorities and no one will be excluded because he cannot raise the fee.

There are in addition two PHAB clubs which meet weekly in London: at the Oval House, Kennington, SE11 on Thursday evenings, and at 30 Devonshire Street on Monday evenings.

PRE-SCHOOL PLAYGROUPS ASSOCIATION, 87a, Borough High Street, SE1 [407 – 7815].

Playgroups give valuable play experience to children between three and five years old, usually for two and a half hours, two or three times a week. They also help mothers to understand more fully the needs of their children and help to break down isolation by involving them with others in a community venture.

The groups are normally held in church or similar halls or in private houses. All mothers are encouraged to take an active part whether this is helping at play sessions or doing other necessary jobs for the benefit of the group. Playgroups are essentially a community effort and a place where mothers and children are welcomed together.

Many local authorities now run playgroup courses, and further information can be obtained from local education offices. Sometimes this is an evening course, but in London courses are often held during the daytime, sometimes with a playgroup attached where pre-school children can stay whilst their mothers are attending the course. For specific details about activities in London contact Inner London Pre-School Playgroups Association, 47 Denison House, 296 Vauxhall Bridge Road, London, SW1.

Membership of the Pre-School Playgroups Association costs £1·50 a year, which includes ten editions of the magazine *Contact*. Other helpful publications available include *How to Start a Playgroup* and *Playgroup Activities*.

ROYAL ASSOCIATION IN AID OF THE DEAF AND DUMB, 7 Armstrong Road, W3 [743 – 6187].

The Association needs volunteer help, particularly in its work with blind-deaf people, both help in clubs, with transport to and from clubs, and with home visiting. Clerical and secretarial assistance and help with fund-raising are also welcomed.

ROYAL NATIONAL INSTITUTE FOR THE BLIND, 224 Great Portland Street, W1 [387 – 5251].

This Institute has a team of volunteers who can be called upon either for day or evening work with blind people. The work may consist of reading for pleasure, research or study; giving secretarial or clerical help in reading and answering letters; acting as an escort or guide on a pleasure or shopping expedition. Blind people can get in touch with these and other services for the blind through the welfare department of their local authority.

ROYAL SOCIETY FOR THE PREVENTION OF CRUELTY TO ANIMALS, 105 Jermyn Street, SW1 [930 – 0971].

The purpose of the RSPCA is to check cruelty to animals and to promote their welfare. It has a uniformed inspectorate to investigate cases of cruelty and it runs animal clinics and shelters. Members of RSPCA branches raise money for the support of these activities and work in close cooperation with their local inspectors.

ST JOHN AMBULANCE BRIGADE, London District Headquarters, 29 Weymouth Street, W1 [580 – 6762].

The Brigade provides first-aid and welfare services. The first-aid work is carried out at national and public functions, and in accidents and emergencies. The welfare services include auxiliary nursing services in hospitals, to the chronic sick at home, and to the elderly and disabled. Volunteers must pass the Brigade's examination in first-aid, and, for women, the one in nursing, before being accepted for this work. An annual re-examination must be passed. Volunteers not wishing to take examinations may serve as auxiliaries in work other than nursing and first-aid, such as help with hospital libraries, sick visiting, etc. Brigade members must attend at least twelve divisional instruction meetings per year and give as much time as possible to the work.

SALVATION ARMY, 101 Queen Victoria Street, EC4 [236 – 5222].

The aim of the Salvation Army in its own words is 'to fight sin and sickness, need and want, insecurity and doubt, disaster and hopelessness . . . with the Bible and the love of God in people's hearts' – and also with very hard day-to-day service.

The Salvation Army helps all people in trouble. It has approved schools, homes and hostels for unmarried mothers and their babies, hostels for the homeless, treatment centres for alcoholics, prison after-care services, a missing persons bureau with world-wide links, and an anti-suicide bureau among its many cares. In this work it needs help with the mothers and babies, with children, with the aged and handicapped, and in community centres.

THE SAMARITANS, St Stephen's Church, Walbrook, EC4 [626 – 9000].

The Samaritans help the suicidal and despairing. Callers may remain anonymous and be befriended or counselled only over the telephone if they so wish. Volunteers are recruited for the work of counselling. They are asked for references, interviewed, and observed in preparation discussion groups. If accepted at this stage, they are put on six months' probation before final ac-ceptance. For the sake of clients, they must be willing to promise absolute discretion, and to work under direction. The age range for volunteers is from 18 years upwards.

SHELTER, 86 Strand, WC2 [836 – 2051].

Shelter is the National Campaign for the Homeless. It raises funds to provide accommodation for families who are homeless, overcrowded or living in slums. Shelter Groups raise money, give publicity to the problem of homelessness and carry out pressure activities to relieve unnecessary housing injustices in their own area.

Because Shelter works through voluntary housing associations which attract improvement subsidies, local authority loans and voluntary effort, each £1 raised for Shelter buys £8 worth of housing.

Shelter publishes a pamphlet *A Home of Your Own* (12½p) to advise young people on how *not* to become homeless.

SOCIAL SERVICES DEPARTMENTS of London Boroughs (inquiries to appropriate town hall).

The Children's Departments advise and help families to pro-mote the welfare of children and prevent the break-up of families. When parents are unable to provide for their children, and this may be in an everyday emergency such as a mother having to go into hospital, the Council acts as parents and provides homes for these children. The departments maintain Children's Homes and arrange fostering and adoptions.

Volunteers may help by assisting trained social workers, offering hospitality and a continuing interest to children in Homes, acting as foster parents for long or short periods and helping the children's homes to be an integrated part of their community.

SOCIAL WORK ADVISORY SERVICE, 26 Bloomsbury Way, WC1.

If you are considering social work as a career, you can write to the Advisory Service for information about different types of social work and the necessary qualifications for them.

TASK FORCE, Clifford House, Edith Villas, W14 [603 – 0271].

Task Force aims to provide a service to the community, of the kind which young volunteers can give: friendship and practical help to the elderly, lonely and disabled; and local community projects. Task Force works for direct involvement of young people (aged 15–30) in the problems of their own community. There are ten local centres through which your energies and time can be linked to the needs of the community.

TERRITORIAL AND ARMY VOLUNTEER RESERVE, Duke of York's Headquarters, King's Road, SW3 [730 – 8131].

A high proportion of Britain's Regular Army consists of troops in fighting units with only a limited number of supporting units. Thus organized, it is capable of dealing with normal emergencies but, if a serious situation necessitated major military operations overseas, additional and immediate support would be required. The Territorial and Army Volunteer Reserve (T & AVR) is a reserve of highly trained and well-equipped units and individuals who can take their place alongside units and men of the Regular Army when necessary.

You can join the T & AVR at seventeen and may sign on for two, three or four years, which is then renewable. You may apply to resign at any time. Each year you must undergo certain obligatory training including fifteen days' continuous camp, including weekends, and about fourteen days' out-of-camp training. Some of this training takes place abroad. An annual training bounty is paid for completed service which can amount to £85 per year.

The Queen Alexandra's Royal Army Nursing Corps (QARANC) needs qualified nursing and medical auxiliary volunteers and the Women's Royal Army Corps (WRAC) needs signallers, telephonists and clerks in the Royal Signal Regiments. Training and call-out liability for women is the same as for men.

TOC H, 15 Trinity Square, EC3 [709 – 0472].

Toc H was started after the First World War to continue the spirit of fellowship and service which people had experienced during the war, and to use it to serve the community. Volunteers work with old people, children, refugees, the mentally handicapped, ex-prisoners and others. Summer Toc H Projects include play schemes, work with housing associations, and help with holidays for disabled adults and retarded children.

VOLUNTEER EMERGENCY SERVICE, 52 Mollison Drive, Wallington, Surrey [647 – 6183].

The VES provides an emergency service for such things as carrying blood and medical supplies for doctors and hospitals, helping other organizations and the elderly with transport problems and emergencies. Volunteers are needed who have any form of transport 'from a moped to a pantechnicon', and also to help with the administration of the service.

WHAT?, Bedford Chambers, Covent Garden, WC2 [836 – 8967].

When you say, 'Why don't they . . .?', What?, the journal of the National Innovations Centre, wants to know. Send them your ideas, inventions or suggestions. They will, where appropriate, investigate, develop and publish them in the quarterly journal. There are £5 quarterly prizes for the most constructive suggestions. Larger grants are from time to time awarded to assist people to make a preliminary study of the viability of a project or to put a suggestion into practice. Subscription to What? is £1 a year.

WOMEN'S ROYAL VOLUNTARY SERVICE WINGED FELLOWSHIP, 17 Old Park Lane, W1 [499 – 6040].

The WRVS have two Holiday Homes, one in Essex and one in Surrey, where physically handicapped people can have a fortnight's holiday at most times during the year. Most of the staff at the homes are volunteers between 17 and 60, who work for periods of a week, fortnight or longer and receive board and lodging and fares if required. This work is followed up through an annual newsletter, giving the disabled and volunteers news of each other.

YOUTH CLUBS. The following organizations need volunteers who can give specialized instruction in clubs (dancing, art, drama, sport, etc.); general and administrative help with running clubs; and help at weekends with activities such as pot-holing, rock climbing, and preparation for the Duke of Edinburgh's Award Scheme (see p. 54).

LONDON FEDERATION OF BOYS' CLUBS, 121 Kennington Park Road, SE11 [735 – 7083].

LONDON UNION OF YOUTH CLUBS, St Anne's House, Venn Street, SW4 [622 – 4347].

NATIONAL ASSOCIATION OF YOUTH CLUBS, Devonshire Street House, 30 Devonshire Street, W1 [935 – 2941].

PROTECTION OF THE ENVIRONMENT

BRITISH TRUST FOR CONSERVATION VOLUNTEERS, Zoological Gardens, Regent's Park, NW1 [722 – 7112].

The Conservation Volunteers work to conserve the plant and animal life of the countryside in nature reserves, national parks, commons and other land. Typical tasks include clearing undergrowth, planting trees, digging out ponds and laying out new nature trails. Surveying, mapping and recording are also undertaken.

You must be at least 16 to join the Volunteers. Weekend, day and residential tasks are organized throughout the year, the longer, weekly or fortnightly camps taking place in the Easter and summer holiday periods.

COUNCIL FOR THE PROTECTION OF RURAL ENGLAND, 4 Hobart Place, SW1 [235 – 4771].

The objects of the Council are to protect the beauty of the countryside from disfigurement and injury, to act as a centre for information and advice on matters affecting the protection of rural scenery, and to rouse public opinion to an understanding of the importance of this work. The Council works through its branches to promote these aims. The Greater London branch has become the Headquarters group and is concerned with fund-raising and training members to help, report and advise on conservation matters in and around London.

THE FAUNA PRESERVATION SOCIETY, The Zoological Gardens, Regent's Park, NW1 [586 – 0872].

The Society was founded in 1903, and its principal aim is to save the world's endangered wildlife. It works closely with the World Wildlife Fund. The annual subscription is £3, and membership entitles you to attend the Society's regular meetings, and join in all its other activities, such as the overseas tours, Oryx Tours, guided by specialists and giving members an opportunity to see the wildlife of other parts of the world. You also receive three free copies a year of *Oryx*, the Society's journal.

INLAND WATERWAYS ASSOCIATION, 114 Regent's Park Road, NW1 [586 – 2510].

If you look at a map of London, you can see meandering through it, from Greenford to the Thames opposite Greenwich, London's canal, the Regent's Canal. Unless you know where it is you are seldom aware of it.

Through the work of the Inland Waterways Association you can take part in the life of this and the many other canals in Britain. In the summer the Association runs trips, tow-path walks and visits. In the winter there are lectures and visits. The Association organizes work parties to rehabilitate stretches of canal. Information about these appears in their *Bulletin* and the *Navvies' Notebook* which are issued to members. The reports of working parties mention removing anything up to 1,000 tons of rubbish from a canal over a weekend, and using 300 tons of rubble to build an access road.

Membership is £2·50 a year including a branch subscription of 40p a year. A husband and wife can join for £3·50 and Junior members under 18 years for £1·05. Write for details and a list of waterway publications.

NATIONAL SOCIETY FOR CLEAN AIR, Field House, Breams Buildings, EC4 [242 – 5038].

The objects of the Society are to promote clean air in the United Kingdom by creating an informed public opinion on its importance. Members work through divisional groups and are entitled to receive assistance and information on problems relating to air pollution.

SOCIETY FOR THE PROMOTION OF NATURE RESERVES, The Manor House, Alford, Lincolnshire.

The Society is the central body to which the County Naturalists' Trusts and the Nature Conservation Trusts are affiliated. There are County Naturalists' Trusts in all the counties surrounding London. Don't think that because you live in London nature reserves must necessarily be out of your reach. Your interest and help are needed wherever you live.

Membership of the Trusts is open to all, and the minimum annual subscription is normally £1. For a list of addresses of the County headquarters write to the Society's headquarters at Alford.

SERVICE TO THE
INTERNATIONAL COMMUNITY

BRITISH VOLUNTEER PROGRAMME, 26 Bedford Square, WC1 [636 – 4066].

The four societies within the BVP recruit, select and train about 1,500 volunteers a year for overseas service. Qualified volunteers (teachers, doctors and medical auxiliaries, engineers, agriculturalists, librarians, accountants, social workers, etc.) are needed in countries in Africa, Asia, Latin America and the Caribbean and Pacific areas. Volunteers receive board and lodging and pocket money. Their return fares, a small outfit allowance, social security payments and a modest resettlement grant are paid. The minimum period of service is one year, but, from the point of view of the receiving country this is often inefficient and unsatisfactory, and volunteers prepared to offer at least fifteen to twenty-four months are encouraged.

You can apply to the BVP who will redirect your application to one of the sending agencies or you can write direct to one of the sending agencies. One application is sufficient to ensure consideration by all the organizations, but if you are not accepted by the selection panel of one agency, you cannot be reconsidered by that or another agency for twelve months. The sending agencies are:

Catholic Institute for International Relations, 41 Holland Park, W11 [727 – 3195].

International Voluntary Service, 91 High Street, Harlesden, NW10 [965 – 1446].

United Nations Association International Service, 93 Albert Embankment, SE1 [735 – 4431]. Some UNA volunteers are serving directly with UN specialized agencies – FAO, UN High Commission for Refugees, WHO, UNESCO, etc.

Voluntary Service Overseas, 14 Bishops Bridge Road, W2 [262 – 2485]. VSO also has a scheme for school leavers, qualified apprentices, farm institute trainees and police cadets.

CHRISTIAN AID, 2 Sloane Gardens, SW1 [730 – 0614].

The purpose of Christian Aid is to finance and undertake practical schemes which 'raise the stricken and deprived to their feet'. The origins of its structure are rooted in the churches, but its funds go where they are most needed, regardless of religion. Money for projects comes from individual donations and group fund-raising. Group work is centred especially on the annual Christian Aid Week, now a nation-wide campaign conducted by over 2,000 interdenominational committees in England, Scotland, Wales and Ireland.

OXFAM, 12 Crane Court, Fleet Street, EC4 [353 – 5701]; 172 Archway Road, N6 [340 – 4891]; 757 Romford Road, E12 [553 – 0836]; 333 Upper Richmond Road West, SW14 [876 – 3399]; 27 Mason's Hill, Bromley, Kent [460 – 1991].

Oxfam exists to help the poor and needy in developing countries and to give aid at times of disaster and emergency. Their most important work is in development projects – helping people to help themselves.

There are Oxfam groups in most areas of London. They consist of individuals who work together to raise money for overseas projects. Part of their work is to encourage informed and sympathetic public opinion towards overseas aid. In many areas there are Oxfam shops, where gifts of books, clothing, china, or anything are sold to raise funds. These shops are staffed by volunteers and sell articles donated by the public.

ROYAL COMMONWEALTH SOCIETY, 18 Northumberland Avenue, WC2 [930 – 6733].

The Royal Commonwealth Society concerns itself with the evolution, development and relationships of the lands and peoples of the Commonwealth. Members have the use of the club premises in Northumberland Avenue where there are a variety of activities, informational and social. The Commonwealth Library has been built up over the last century and has over 400,000 items ranging from original documents to the latest periodicals. There are regular lunch-time and evening meetings and conferences, and a varied programme of social events (parties to the Derby, to Glyndebourne, to concerts, etc., and activities arranged by members). Membership fees are £4 a year (17–24 years), £8 a year (25–30) and £16 a year for full membership.

UNITED NATIONS ASSOCIATION, 93 Albert Embankment, SE1 [735 – 0181].

The United Nations Association was founded to support the United Nations Organization in its peace-keeping and humanitarian roles, through the work of an informed body of opinion in its member countries.

Through UNA International Service you may volunteer for work camps or give a longer period of service either at home or abroad. The London branch (London Regional Office, 1 Hill Place, W1 [734 – 0368]) organizes meetings, discussions, conferences and many social and fund-raising events. There is an annual subscription which varies between 50p and £1 depending on the services you require.

WAR ON WANT, 2b The Grove, W5 [567 – 1429].

War on Want seeks to create sympathy and support in Britain for the needs of the developing countries of the world. A personal link is maintained between projects in the developing countries and supporters in Britain. Money is raised for overseas projects through appeals and gift shops manned by volunteer helpers.

PRESSURE GROUPS AND POLITICS

THE AFRICA BUREAU, 2 Arundel Street, WC2 [836 – 4585].

The aims of the Bureau are to improve understanding in Britain about current African events and problems; to promote British policies that will assist social and economic development in Africa; to oppose racial tyrannies in Africa; and to promote the achievement of non-discriminatory majority rule in Africa. To this end the Bureau publishes pamphlets, a journal and other literature. More particularly, it offers an information service and generates interest and participation by establishing groups of people anxious to be informed about Africa and helpful towards it.

Annual membership is £2 (including receipt of Bureau pamphlets); annual subscription for bi-monthly journal, *Africa Digest*, is £2, students £1.

AGIT-PROP INFORMATION, 160 North Gower Street, NW1 [387 – 5406].

Agit-Prop is an information centre for left-wing political and action groups. They will advise on running a campaign, and they publish leaflets on how to start and manage a local journal, how to run poster workshops, how to get together and present street plays, how to start a film society, and generally how to organize a pressure group. They also produce a directory listing contact addresses of over 500 British left-groups for activists.

AMNESTY INTERNATIONAL, Turnagain Lane, Farringdon Street, EC4 [236 – 0111].

Amnesty International has branches in many parts of the world devoted to championing the rights of individuals as stated in the UN Declaration of Human Rights. It is concerned with assisting people who have been imprisoned or persecuted for their beliefs, political or religious. Each Amnesty group (there are over twenty in London) 'adopts' three 'prisoners of conscience' from different parts of the world and works on their behalf – to press for their release, to help them and their families, and to get publicity for their case. The groups raise money for this work and for the overall work of the organization. There are also schemes by which individuals can bring pressure on behalf of individual prisoners.

ANTI-APARTHEID MOVEMENT, 89 Charlotte Street, W1 [580 – 5311].

This Movement publicizes the facts about apartheid and racialism in Southern Africa. It campaigns against British involvement in and collaboration with the white minority rule in Southern Africa by distributing information, providing speakers for public meetings, and organizing demonstrations, conferences and other meetings. The Movement lobbies the government directly, campaigns in and through the trade-union movement, the political parties and to the general public. It urges a ban on emigration to South Africa; presses for economic sanctions, particularly against the illegal régime in Rhodesia; urges the maintenance of the arms embargo to South Africa; calls for a total boycott on cultural and sporting activities based on racial selection; works for an end to NATO association with Portuguese African policies; works for self-determination and independence for Angola, Mozambique, Guine-Bissau, South West Africa, Rhodesia and South Africa.

BRITISH HUMANIST ASSOCIATION, 13 Prince of Wales Terrace, W8 [937 – 2341].

Humanists believe that this world is all we have or need and that we should try to live full, happy lives and help to make it easier for other people to do the same.

The work of the BHA includes political pressure for social reform, specialist research, social action (e.g. housing for the elderly, counselling, adoption) and support of overseas projects. The BHA arranges courses and conferences and publishes a magazine. Local groups arrange programmes of social and educational events and projects.

CAMPAIGN FOR NUCLEAR DISARMAMENT, 14 Gray's Inn Road, WC1 [242 – 3872].

CND was formed in 1958 to rouse people to the dangers of nuclear war and to secure the abolition of all nuclear weapons before they destroy humanity. It campaigns for unilateral nuclear disarmament by Britain, and the abandonment of nuclear weapons by all other countries, as a lead to general disarmament. Its policies include British withdrawal from NATO and increased support of the United Nations. CND campaigns for money to be spent on people, not weapons.

Local CND groups hold meetings so that members may form an informed public opinion. Once a year, at Easter, CND has its national demonstration, which in a very few years has become a traditional British event, but continues to be an event with a purpose.

CAMPAIGN AGAINST RACIAL DISCRIMINATION, 23 St George's House, Toynbee Hall, Commercial Street, E1 [247 – 5581].

CARD is a multi-racial organization committed to achieving equality of opportunity in Britain regardless of colour, race, religion or national origin. Local branches of CARD work against racial prejudice and discrimination at the community level. Activities depend on the problems of each area, but will cover such things as working with tenants to establish their rights, voter registration, fair employment policies, lobbying councillors and MPs and testing cases of suspected discrimination.

COMMON MARKET. During Britain's negotiating sorties to join the Common Market a number of organizations have been formed, either to press for or to oppose entry.

For entry:

UNITED EUROPE ASSOCIATION, 78 Chandos House, Buckingham Gate, SW1 [799 – 2922].

This is the membership body of the European Movement. Membership of the European Movement is open to all individuals subscribing to the ideal of European Union both economically and politically on the basis of an enlarged Common Market with effective and democratically controlled institutions. Members work towards an informed pro-Common Market opinion. There are in addition a number of organizations with a professional membership which work through the United Europe Association representing management, solicitors, students, teachers, etc.

Against entry:

ANTI-COMMON MARKET LEAGUE, 79b Iverna Court, W8 [937 – 7686].

The League was formed in 1961 to campaign against Britain

signing the Treaty of Rome and joining the European Economic Community. Members work through local groups.

COMMON MARKET SAFEGUARDS CAMPAIGN, 55 Park Lane, W1 [629 – 8741].

The Campaign supplies information on the Common Market and arranges speakers and petitions, with particular reference to safeguards for Britain should she enter the Common Market.

KEEP BRITAIN OUT CAMPAIGN, 5 Mertoun Terrace, Seymour Place, W1 [402 – 5618].

The Campaign's main objective is to make vocal, both in this country and in Europe, the opposition to the Common Market. Debates and meetings are arranged.

CONNOLLY ASSOCIATION, 283 Gray's Inn Road, WC1 [837 – 4826].

The aim of the Connolly Association is to organize Irish men and women resident in Britain for the defence of their interests and, in particular, to win support for the struggle of the Irish for a united Republic. It is an organization based on the teachings of the socialist, James Connolly, and on working-class interests, though it does not think that other classes cannot share interests with the working class. The Association publishes a monthly paper, the *Irish Democrat*, and runs the Irish Democrat Book Centre which is open every Wednesday evening and from 10 a.m. to 3 p.m. on Saturdays.

CO-OPERATIVE PARTY, 158 Buckingham Palace Road, SW1 [730 – 8187].

The Co-operative Party is the political arm of the Co-operative Movement. Its aim is to represent consumer interests and propagate co-operative principles. It works in close harmony with the Labour Party.

INDEPENDENT LABOUR PARTY, 197 King's Cross Road, WC1 [837 – 2445].

The ILP was founded in the 1890s as a forerunner of the Labour Party, and it is one of the oldest socialist parties in the country. Separate from the Labour Party since 1933, it continues to contest seats in local and general elections and to campaign for a socialist society with total public ownership and workers' control. It combines with similar socialist organizations in campaigns.

There are local party groups in London which can be contacted through the national office. The ILP publishes the weekly paper, *Socialist Leader*.

INTERNATIONAL SOCIALISTS, 6 Cotton Gardens, E2 [739 – 1878].

The IS is a revolutionary Marxist organization in the Trotskyist tradition. It believes that society cannot be reformed, only totally transformed on the basis of workers' power and the continuous democracy of workers' councils. It campaigns to help build a new mass socialist party openly challenging for state power.

It has an active membership through its eighty local branches, with emphasis on industrial work but also with strong roots in the student movement. IS publishes a weekly paper, *Socialist Worker* and a bi-monthly magazine, *International Socialist*.

LONDON SOCIETY OF ANARCHIST GROUPS, 846 Whitechapel High Street, E1 [247 – 9249].

Anarchists believe in a society organized by the people comprising it, with no authority, and thereby no coercion. Therefore most anarchist work is directed against the State as it is organized, and towards showing people, by example and by written work, how they can take control of their own lives and the direction that they should take. Groups in different areas of London decide their own methods of working: in Hornsey they publish a broadsheet and there have been street theatre activities; in East London the group have published leaflets and campaigned for support for striking council workers. There is a weekly public meeting at the LSAG office. Information about group activities can be obtained by phoning the LSAG office in the afternoon or evening.

NATIONAL COUNCIL FOR CIVIL LIBERTIES, 152 Camden High Street, NW1 [485 – 9497].

The NCCL is concerned with individual civil liberties and the rights of political, religious, racial and other minorities in Britain. Cases submitted to the NCCL are investigated and where an injustice is seen to be done representations are made on behalf of the complainant. On broader issues of citizens' rights, the NCCL campaigns for law reform.

Members of the NCCL participate in the work by acting as observers at political and industrial demonstrations and meetings, attending court cases, acting as representatives of mental-health patients, and submitting evidence to the NCCL of any abuses of civil liberties that come to their attention. People with specialized experience in social work, trade unions or the law are especially needed, but help with routine clerical work, public speaking, fund-raising, etc. is always welcome.

PEACE PLEDGE UNION, 6 Endsleigh Street, WC1 [387 – 5501].

The PPU is a pacifist organization, founded in 1934, dedicated to creating a peaceful world society through influencing individuals and national and international policies. It is non-party and non-sectarian. All members sign the Peace Pledge renouncing war. It has groups throughout the country concerned with discussion and public education and, as an organization, it co-operates with other peace movements in demonstrations and delegations.

PPU is the British Section of War Resisters' International (Headquarters: 3 Caledonian Road, N1 [837 – 3860], a federal body which has affiliated organizations in thirty-nine countries. *Peace News*, a pacifist weekly newspaper (editorial office: 5 Caledonian Road, N1 [837 – 4473]) is an associated publication of WRI.

POLITICAL PARTIES. If you want to join a political party you can contact the headquarters of that party, who will put you in touch with your constituency party, or you can contact the constituency party direct. The main function of a political party is to fight elections, but between elections a great deal of educational, social and continuing work goes on.

COMMUNIST PARTY OF GREAT BRITAIN, 16 King Street, WC2 [836 – 2151].

CONSERVATIVE AND UNIONIST PARTY, 32 Smith Square, SW1 [222 – 9000].

LIBERAL PARTY, 7 Exchange Court, Strand, WC2 [208 – 0701].

LABOUR PARTY, Transport House, Smith Square, SW1 [834 – 9434].

In addition to the four main and other minor political parties there are two well-known political research and discussion groups: the BOW GROUP, 240 High Holborn, WC1 [405 – 0878] and the FABIAN SOCIETY, 11 Dartmouth Street, SW1 [930 – 3077].

The Bow Group is Conservative, the Fabian Society is committed to the principles of democratic socialism. Neither adopts any particular collective standpoint. They both exist to generate discussion and research, through lectures and study groups, into political ideas and policies. Both publish pamphlets and newsletters about their activities and run weekend and summer schools.

SOCIETY FOR ANGLO-CHINESE UNDERSTANDING LTD, 24 Warren Street, W1 [387 – 0074].

SACU was founded in 1965 to promote friendship and understanding between the people of Britain and China. The Society holds regular meetings and film shows, and has a list of speakers available for meetings. A monthly journal, *China Now* (5p), is available from the Society and some bookshops. Annual subscription to SACU is £1·50, full-time students 62½p.

THE SOCIETY FOR CULTURAL RELATIONS WITH THE USSR, 320 Brixton Road, SW9 [274 – 2282].

SCR aims to increase understanding and friendship between Great Britain and the USSR by providing facilities for an exchange of views and information. It has a library of books and periodicals on all aspects of Soviet life, and current issues of many Soviet journals and newspapers. The Society's own magazine, the *Anglo-Soviet Journal* (30p) appears three times a year and is sent free to members. Membership fee is £2·50, students and pensioners 55p.

The Society also organizes meetings, discussion groups, specialist tours, an annual Easter vacation Russian language course, with Russian teachers, and a Russian language summer vacation course in Moscow. For details of the current programme write to the Secretary.

SOCIETY FOR TEACHERS OPPOSED TO PHYSICAL PUNISHMENT, 12 Lawn Road, NW3

STOPP is a pressure group of teachers and parents which

campaigns against the use of physical punishment in schools. Their aims are to urge their cause in the teachers' unions, to collect information on and promote research into the effects of physical punishment, to give professional advice to individuals, to promote local discussion groups and public lectures, and to put pressure on authorities with the ultimate aim of getting a private member's bill on the matter through parliament.

THE SOUTH PLACE ETHICAL SOCIETY, Conway Hall, Red Lion Square, WC1 [242 – 8033].

The author of a leaflet entitled *What is the South Place Ethical Society?* describes it as being, among other things, 'a gathering of people in an accepting climate for difference, where members share their concern for human and philosophic understanding, education and social action; yet feel free to find their own answers'. To this end the Society organizes regular lectures, discussions, Sunday evening concerts and social activities. Membership (annual subscription 62½p minimum) entitles you to attend any meetings, to receive the journal published monthly, and to use the Society's library at Conway Hall. Non-members are welcomed at meetings.

WOMEN'S LIBERATION WORKSHOP, 127 Lower Marsh Street, SE1 [928 – 6125].

WLW believes that women in our society are oppressed, underpaid, commercially exploited by the media, and often lacking in legal status. WLW seeks to devise methods to change the inferior status of women. Small groups are the basic units of the movement, so that WLW incorporates a wide group of opinions and plans for action. The magazine, *Shrew*, is produced by a different group each month.

RELIGIOUS ORGANIZATIONS

The list given here is of centres where you can get information about a particular faith and its work in the London area.

BAPTIST UNION OF GREAT BRITAIN AND IRELAND, 4 Southampton Row, WC1 [405 – 2045].

THE BRITISH COUNCIL OF CHURCHES, see p. 51.

THE BUDDHIST SOCIETY, 58 Eccleston Square, SW1 [828 – 1313].

Information is available from the librarian between 2 p.m. and 6 p.m. only.

CHRISTIAN SCIENTIST: District Manager, Christian Science Committees on Publication for Great Britain and Northern Ireland, Ingersoll House, 9 Kingsway, WC2 [836 – 2808].

CHURCH OF ENGLAND: Inquiry Centre of the Church of England, Church House, Deans Yard, SW1 [222 – 9011].

CHURCH OF SCOTLAND: St Columba's Church of Scotland Office, Pont Street, SW1 [584 – 2321].

THE CONGREGATIONAL CHURCH IN ENGLAND AND WALES, Livingstone House, 11 Carteret Street, SW1 [930 – 0061].

FREE CHURCH FEDERAL COUNCIL, 27 Tavistock Square, WC1 [387 – 8413].

Inquiries will be answered on behalf of the Baptists, the Congregationalists, the Methodists, the Presbyterian Church of England, the Presbyterian Church of Wales, the Independent Methodist Churches, the Wesleyan Reform Union, the Moravian Church, the Countess of Huntingdon's Connection, the Churches of Christ, the Free Church of England.

GREEK ORTHODOX METROPOLIS OF THYATIRA AND GREAT BRITAIN, 5 Craven Hill, W2 [723 – 4787].

THE HINDU CENTRE, 39 Grafton Terrace, NW5 [485 – 8200].

ISLAMIC CULTURAL CENTRE AND LONDON CENTRAL MOSQUE, 146 Park Road, NW8 [723 – 7611].

BOARD OF DEPUTIES OF BRITISH JEWS, Woburn House, Upper Woburn Place, WC1 [387 – 3952].

LUTHERAN COUNCIL OF GREAT BRITAIN, 8 Collingham Gardens, SW5 [373 – 1141].

METHODIST CHURCH PRESS AND INFORMATION SERVICE, Room 73, 1 Central Buildings, Central Hall, Westminster, SW1 [930 – 1751].

MORAVIAN CHURCH, 5 Muswell Hill, N10 [883 – 3409].

PENTECOSTAL BRITISH FELLOWSHIP, 51 Newington Causeway, SE1 [407 – 1879].

PRESBYTERIAN CHURCH OF ENGLAND, 86 Tavistock Place, WC1 [837 – 0862].

QUAKERS: FRIENDS HOME SERVICE COMMITTEE, Friends House, Euston Road, NW1 [387 – 3601].

ROMAN CATHOLIC: Catholic Central Library and Information Centre, 47 Francis Street, SW1 [834 – 6128].

SALVATION ARMY, 101 Queen Victoria Street EC4 [236 – 5222].

SEVENTH-DAY ADVENTISTS, New Gallery, Evangelistic Centre, 123 Regent Street, W1 [734 – 8888].

SIKH TEMPLE, 62 Queensdale Road, W11 [603 – 2789].

SPIRITUALIST ASSOCIATION OF GREAT BRITAIN, 33 Belgrave Square, SW1 [235 – 3351].

STUDENT CHRISTIAN MOVEMENT, Annandale, North End Road, NW11 [455 – 2311].

UNITARIAN CHURCHES IN LONDON, Essex Hall, Essex Street, WC2 [240 – 2384].

4

SPORTS

There are arrangements in London for participation in every type of sport, outdoors and indoors, team and individual. Some facilities are free or very cheap, some can be expensive. Here we are mainly concerned with the cheaper ones and those that are more readily available. There are also many opportunities for watching other people participating, both amateurs and top professionals.

You can find out about the facilities for the sport which interests you in a variety of ways: through local newspapers, from posters on the underground, from friends, from the *British Club Year Book and Directory* at your local library, or through your local authority.

In the 1970 issue of *Floodlight*, the Inner London Education Authority's booklet of evening classes, training sessions were available for the following: angling, archery, badminton, boxing, canoeing, and canoe building, climbing, cricket, cycling, fencing, Association football, Rugby football, golf, hockey, judo, keep fit, medau, netball, navigation for yachtsmen, roller skating, rowing, sailing, swimming, table tennis, volleyball, weight-lifting and wrestling.

A very useful source of information is:

CENTRAL COUNCIL OF PHYSICAL RECREATION (London and S.E. Region), 160 Great Portland Street, W1 [580 – 9092].

Among the functions of the CCPR is that of giving 'help and advice to individuals and organizations in the field of physical recreation'. It runs an information service with a small subscription which brings you details of training courses, demonstrations and lectures on all kinds of sports. The CCPR will put you in touch with the local organizers of any sport which interests you. The CCPR also runs week-long summer courses and some weekend courses at the National Sports Centres. A list of these courses at various levels (elementary, intermediate, advanced, coaching) is available.

The National Sports Centres are:

CRYSTAL PALACE SPORTS CENTRE, Norwood, SE19 [778 – 0131].

The Centre was built for the use of all who are interested in sport and is a training centre for clubs, coaches and individuals. It contains swimming, diving and teaching pools with seating for 1,700 spectators; an indoor arena for tennis, basketball or netball with seating for 1,300 spectators; four badminton and six squash courts; an indoor cricket school; a stadium with 12,000 seats, with grass pitch, a Tartan track and full-scale lighting for evening training; outdoor tennis and basketball courts; an artificial ski slope. In addition there is a hostel for 140 people, a restaurant, and recreation and lecture rooms.

You can become an Authorized User of the National Sports Centre for a fee of £1 a year for adults, 25p a year for school-children. This gives you entry to the Centre only and there is then a charge for use of the various facilities. As the Centre's main function is to provide facilities for training courses and competitive events, the times when facilities are available to Authorized Users may be altered to allow for these main functions. The charges for the use of facilities and times when they are available are approximately as follows:

Swimming, 10p a session; weekdays 12–2 p.m., weekends 9 a.m.–5 p.m.

Squash, 37½p for one court for half an hour; weekdays 12–2 p.m. and 4–10 p.m., weekends 9 a.m.–5 p.m.

Lawn tennis, 25p per hour per court unlit or 50p per hour per court when floodlit; weekdays 9 a.m.–10 p.m., weekends 9 a.m.– 5 p.m.

Athletics, 10p per session; weekdays 9 a.m.–10 p.m., weekends 9 a.m.–5 p.m. The track is also available under floodlights on Tuesdays and Thursdays from 7 to 9 p.m.

Badminton courts, 40p per hour without lights and 60p per hour with lights. Courts are available by arrangement when not being used for training courses.

Judo, table tennis and trampolining instruction is available at 18p per session. Details are available through the Centre.

Weight-training is available, only under supervision/instruction, between 7 and 9.30 p.m. on Mondays, Wednesdays, and Fridays. The cost is 18p per session.

Ski-training is available between October and April. A leaflet is available explaining the arrangements for beginners and for practice sessions for skiers with some experience.

Bookings for squash, lawn tennis and badminton courts should be made in advance, but bookings cannot be taken more than one week beforehand.

There is a regular programme of training courses and other activities at Bisham Abbey, near Marlow, Bucks; Lilleshall Hall, near Newport, Shropshire; and Plas y Brenin National Mountaineering Centre, Capel Curig, North Wales; Holme Perrepoint National Water Sports Centre, near Nottingham.

In this chapter we also list the addresses of over three dozen organizations concerned with sports and games, alphabetically by the name of the game. If the one you are interested in is not listed, the Central Council of Physical Recreation will help you.

LONDON ANGLERS' ASSOCIATION, 50 Elfindale Road, SE24.

There are 840 clubs in the Association for this most popular sport. You can fish in the lakes in many of the Royal and GLC parks (apply to the Parks Superintendent for a permit for Royal parks), in the Thames, and in the Grand Union Canal. A booklet, *Fishing for Londoners*, published by the *Angling Times* will tell you about the rather more obscure spots in and around London.

SOUTHERN COUNTIES ARCHERY ASSOCIATION, 102 Ashgrove Road, Goodmayes, Ilford, Essex.

The Association supplies information about London clubs.

SOUTHERN COUNTIES AMATEUR ATHLETIC ASSOCIATION, 26 Park Crescent, W1 [580 – 3498].

The Association will give information about clubs and training courses in your area. It operates a five-star award scheme for individual proficiency in track and field events. The AAA Championships take place at Wembley Stadium in early July.

BADMINTON ASSOCIATION OF ENGLAND, 81a High Street, Bromley, Kent.

This is the source of information about badminton clubs. All-England Championships are held at Wembley in March.

AMATEUR BASKETBALL ASSOCIATION, London Area Secretary, 32 Longford Avenue, Bedfont, Feltham.

Floodlight lists basketball training courses, but this is an alternative source of information about training and clubs.

BOATING

BRITISH CANOE UNION, 26 Park Crescent, W1 [580 – 4710].

The Union runs a coaching scheme for anyone who wants to learn to canoe properly and safely. It has an advisory service for canoe touring at home and abroad and publishes a guide to inland waterways. There is an annual National Canoe Exhibition early in the year.

ROYAL YACHTING ASSOCIATION, 5 Buckingham Gate, SW1 [828 – 9296].

The Association has a scheme of competency tests. Courses are arranged with the CCPR. Although there are many sailing clubs in the London area, they tend to be heavily over-subscribed with boat-owning members, but many will accept crewing members. The RYA keeps a list of approved sailing schools.

THE NATIONAL SAILING CENTRE, Artic Road, Cowes, Isle of Wight.

Courses at the Centre are based on the RYA proficiency and coaching tests. The Centre is administered by the CCPR in conjunction with the RYA.

AMATEUR ROWING ASSOCIATION, 160 Great Portland Street, W1 [580 – 0854].

If you want to row, the Association will give you addresses of clubs in your area, and will tell you which clubs take beginners.

The Oxford and Cambridge Boat Race is in March or April and there are several regattas in or near London in the summer.

BOAT HIRING. You can hire a row-boat by the hour on the Serpentine in Hyde Park, or in Regent's Park, and also in Alexandra Palace and Crystal Palace parks.

THAMES YOUTH VENTURE. There are many water-pursuit centres in and around London which are open to groups and individuals under 21. If you wish to learn to sail, canoe or row ask the wardens of the centres for details. Courses and competency tests are arranged. The main centres are:

Thames Young Mariners, Ham, Richmond, Surrey [940 – 7052].

Welsh Harp Sailing Base, Cool Oak Lane, NW9 [202 – 6672].

Raven's Ait, Surbiton, Surrey.

Herts Young Mariners, Windmill Lane, Cheshunt, Herts.

Leaside Young Mariners, Spring Lane, E9.

Viscount St David's Floating Youth Club, 15 St Mark's Crescent, NW1 is a privately organized youth centre on the Regent's Canal.

BRITISH TEN PIN BOWLING ASSOCIATION, 212 Lower Clapton Road, E5 [985 – 2115].

The Association will supply a list of forthcoming events. There are nearly a dozen bowling centres in and around London most of which are open daily from 10 a.m.

ABC Bowl, The Broadway, Bexleyheath, Kent [303 – 3325].

ABC Bowl, High Road, Leytonstone, London E11 [539 – 2309].

ABC Bowl, Pinner Road, Harrow, Middlesex [863 – 3491].

ABC Bowl, New Road, Dagenham, Essex [592 – 0347].

Airport Bowl, Bath Road, Harlington, Middlesex [759 – 1396].

Ambassador Lanes, High Street, Edgware, Middlesex [952 – 5296].

Ambassador Lanes, Staines Road, Hounslow, Middlesex [570 – 6967].

Ambassador Lanes, 11–29 Belmont Hill, SE13 [852 – 1119].

Humber Bowl, 30 Shaftesbury Avenue, W1 [437 – 1580].

Wembley Stadium Bowl, Empire Stadium, Wembley [902 – 8560].

LONDON AMATEUR BOXING ASSOCIATION, 67 Central Buildings, 24 Southwark Street, SE1 [407 – 2194].

The Association will put you in touch with local clubs. There are training evenings and inter-club competitions in the boxing season from September to May. The ABA Championships are held in the late spring. *Boxing News* gives details of events in and around London—watch out for programmes at the Royal Albert Hall, Seymour Hall, and the Earls Court Arena.

NATIONAL CRICKET ASSOCIATION, Lord's Cricket Ground, St John's Wood Road, NW8. The Association has a coaching scheme, issuing coaching awards. It will put you in touch with your nearest club.

GOVER CRICKET SCHOOL, 172 East Hill, SW18. [874 – 1796].

Here you can receive coaching at any age, 7 to 70, six days a week. It is wise to book up six weeks in advance during the winter and Easter holidays.

Nets can be booked at several GLC parks. You can watch first-class cricket at Lord's, St John's Wood Road, NW8 and at the Oval, Kennington, SE11 (and you can arrange to watch practices at Lord's and the Oval if you apply in advance [Lord's, 289 – 1300; the Oval, 735 – 2424]), and you can watch village-style cricket at Chiswick Park, Ham Common, Kew Green, Stanmore Green, Holland Park, and Wimbledon Common, throughout the summer. There is a museum of cricket at Lord's which is open daily from 10 a.m. to 4 p.m. except on match days. For the latest Test Match scores dial 160.

CYCLING

There is reported to be a certain camaraderie among London bicyclists as they weave together in and out of the stationary traffic, but to enjoy cycling you need to get out of London, or at least to the outskirts. You can take your bicycle on the Circle, Metropolitan and District lines for half the adult fare. The same applies for cycles taken on British Rail. Bicycles can be hired by the day or the week from Saville's Cycle Stores, 97 Battersea Rise, SW11 [228 – 4279].

BRITISH CYCLING FEDERATION, 26 Park Crescent, W1 [636 – 4602].

The Federation publishes an annual handbook listing clubs and cycle racing events. All affiliated clubs offer facilities for club riding and cycle racing.

There are regular race meetings in the London area from the end of April to the end of August at Paddington Recreation Ground, Randolph Avenue, W9 every Tuesday evening; and

Herne Hill Stadium, Burbage Road, SE24 every Monday evening. There are also a number of other events at both these centres as well as at Danston Park, Bexleyheath and at the National Sports Centre at Crystal Palace during the summer months.

CYCLIST TOURING CLUB, 69 Meadrow, Godalming, Surrey.

The club will send you the name of your nearest group. They also organize training holidays.

DANCING, RHYTHMIC MOVEMENT AND KEEP FIT

Most classes are run by evening institutes, details of which are in *Floodlight*. Leadership training is available and information can be obtained through the CCPR or

COUNTY OF LONDON KEEP FIT ASSOCIATION, 116 Manor Lane, SE12.

THE MEDAU SOCIETY, 220 Balham High Road, SW12 [673 – 7333].

WOMEN'S LEAGUE OF HEALTH AND BEAUTY, Beaumont Cottage, Ditton Close, Thames Ditton, Surrey.

ENGLISH FOLK DANCE AND SONG SOCIETY, Cecil Sharp House, 2 Regent's Park Road, NW1.

For other types of dancing see p. 24.

DRIVING

The Borough of Ealing has a skidpan at the south-west corner of the junction of Western Avenue (A40) and Kensington Road, Northolt, where instruction is given in correcting and controlling skids. The car and instructor are provided. Lessons are given on Mondays to Saturdays between 9.45 a.m. and 4 p.m. They cost £1 and are shared by three people, each person driving for twenty minutes. Apply to the Road Safety Officer, Borough of Ealing, 24 Uxbridge Road, W5 [567 – 3456, extension 529].

AMATEUR FENCING ASSOCIATION, 83 Perham Road, W14 [385 – 7442].

Beginners can obtain tuition either at evening institutes (see *Floodlight*) or clubs. You can get a list of clubs from the above address. The CCPR runs training courses for coaches and other more advanced people.

LONDON SCHOOL OF FLYING, Elstree Aerodrome, Boreham Wood, Herts [953 – 4411].

To be accepted for flying training you must pass a medical examination and you are also encouraged to take a trial lesson, costing about £6. To obtain a pilot's licence you must do a minimum of thirty-five hours solo flying. This is increased to forty hours if it extends over a period of more than six months. The school also gives training in navigation, radio telephony and night flying. When you have your licence, you can hire or buy an aeroplane through the school. The cost of training is about £425 and thereafter the cost of hiring a plane is from £10 an hour upwards, depending on the type wanted.

LONDON FOOTBALL ASSOCIATION, 51 Barking Road, E16 [476 – 1750].

Information is given about clubs where you can play and be coached to play football. The FA Cup Final is held at Wembley in May but it's almost impossible to get tickets unless you are a regular supporter. You can arrange to watch Football League teams practising by applying in advance to: the Manager, Arsenal Stadium (Football Club), Avenall Road, N5 [226 – 3312]; the Manager, Chelsea Football Club, Stamford Bridge, Fulham Road, SW6 [385 – 5545]; the Manager, West Ham United Football Club, Boleyn Ground, Green Street, E13 [472 – 0704]; the Manager, Crystal Palace Football Club, Selhurst Park, SE25 [653 – 2223].

BRITISH GLIDING ASSOCIATION, 75 Victoria Street, SW1 [799 – 7548].

Gliding is an 'all-the-year-round' sport. No previous air experience is needed, nor need you be technically minded. Day and holiday courses are arranged by the Association and the CCPR. Each club will have its own scale of charges, but the entrance fee is likely to be about £5 with an annual subscription of about £10 which includes use of club equipment and facilities and instruction. Launches are paid for as they are taken. A launch by winch or motor car will cost 30p–50p and will give about ten minutes gliding; a launch by aerotow to about 2000 feet will cost about £1·25 and will give fifteen to twenty minutes gliding.

PROFESSIONAL GOLFERS ASSOCIATION, Kennington Oval, SE1 [735 – 8803].

GOLF FOUNDATION, London Scottish Golf Club, Windmill Enclosure, Wimbledon Common, SW19 [789 – 7517].

Both these organizations are concerned with the development of facilities and training for golfers.

The main public golf courses are at Beckenham, Brent Valley (Hanwell), Enfield, Richmond Park and Ruislip. There are also a good number of private clubs within easy reach of central London.

BRITISH AMATEUR GYMNASTICS ASSOCIATION, 23 High Street, Slough, Bucks.

Proficiency award schemes are run by the Association through clubs.

The annual National Gymnastics Championships are held in London as are a number of other national and international events.

HOCKEY ASSOCIATION (Men), 26 Park Crescent, W1 [580 – 4840].

ALL ENGLAND WOMEN'S HOCKEY ASSOCIATION, 45 Doughty Street, WC1 [405 – 7514].

Information about clubs can be obtained from the appropriate County Secretary of whom the Associations will be prepared to give the address.

International matches are played at Wembley Stadium.

BRITISH JUDO ASSOCIATION, 26 Park Crescent, W1 [580 – 7585].

There are many clubs in the London area, with which the Association can put you in touch. Evening institutes also have Judo classes.

ALL ENGLAND WOMEN'S LACROSSE ASSOCIATION, 26 Park Crescent, W1 [636 – 1123].

SOUTH OF ENGLAND MEN'S LACROSSE ASSOCIATION, 282 Cassiobury Drive, Watford, Herts.

Courses in lacrosse are organized both for coaches and for improvement of personal performance. A seven-a-side game suitable for indoors or restricted spaces has recently been introduced.

MOTOR AND MOTOR CYCLE RACING.

Motor race meetings are held at Crystal Palace Circuit, SE19.

Speedway meetings, dates of which are given in the *Speedway Star and News*, are held at Hackney Wick Stadium, Waterden Road, E15 [985 – 4771]; West Ham Stadium, Custom House, E16 [476 – 2441]; and Wimbledon Stadium, Plough Lane, SW17 [946 – 5361].

Stock-car race meetings are held at Harringay Stadium, Green Lane, N4 [800 – 3474]; New Cross Stadium, Hornshay Street, SE15 [639 – 0213]; Walthamstow Stadium, Chingford Road, E4 [527 – 2252]; and Wimbledon Stadium, Plough Lane, SW17 [946 – 5361].

AUTO-CYCLE UNION, 31 Belgrave Square, SW1 [235 – 7636].

The ACU Handbook lists clubs and motor cycle events. The ACU and the Royal Automobile Club run a proficiency training scheme for motor cyclists consisting of twenty-four mainly practical lessons over a three-month period.

BRITISH AUTOMOBILE RACING CLUB, Sutherland House, 5–6 Argyll Street, W1 [437 – 2533].

There are over 100 clubs in the London area and the Club will supply you with a list.

MOUNTAINEERING

THE BRITISH MOUNTAINEERING COUNCIL, 26 Park Crescent, W1 [637 – 1598] and the CCPR will advise beginners in mountaineering and rock climbing and they arrange courses in the London Area. The CCPR's National Centre in Snowdonia offers a variety of training courses.

The Mountain Leadership Training Board runs courses for instructors and leaders.

Weekend rock climbing courses are arranged at Bowles Mountaineering and Outdoor Pursuits Centre, Tunbridge Wells.

ALL ENGLAND NETBALL ASSOCIATION, 26 Park Crescent, W1 [580 – 3459].

The Association will put you in touch with the appropriate County Secretary for information about clubs and coaching. There are a number of netball pitches in the GLC parks which can be hired and a leaflet about these is available from the

GLC Parks Department, Cavell House, 2a Charing Cross Road, WC2.

SOUTH EAST ORIENTEERING ASSOCIATION, Denbigh Lodge, Shalden, Guildford, Surrey.

Orienteering is fast growing in popularity. It is a form of cross-country racing based on the navigation skills of map interpretation and compass work, particularly in forests and woodlands. Although at the highest levels you have to be a good athlete, it is a sport for people of all ages, including families with children. Competitions and training events are held most weekends.

BRITISH PARACHUTE ASSOCIATION, 75 Victoria Street, SW1 [799 – 3760].

The BPA, through its clubs, is responsible for training and safety in parachuting. The minimum age for parachuting is 17 and you must produce a health certificate on a form provided by the club. A weekend's training leading up to a first jump will cost about £10 and subsequent jumps will cost about £1·75. There are half a dozen clubs within fairly easy reach of London.

RIDING

THE GREATER LONDON HORSEMAN'S ASSOCIATION, 74 High Street, Teddington, Middlesex will give advice to anyone who wants to know about opportunities for riding in London.

THE NATIONAL EQUESTRIAN CENTRE, Stoneleigh, Kenilworth, Warwickshire, holds a full programme of lectures, demonstrations and courses.

PONIES OF BRITAIN, Brookside Farm, Ascot, Berkshire, gives advice and information on riding holidays, and publishes a list of holiday centres which have been awarded certificates of approval.

During the year there are a number of events in and around London of interest to those who are interested in the horse. In April there is the Epsom Spring Meeting; in May the Royal Windsor Horse Show at Home Park, Windsor; in June the Derby and the Oaks which are run at Epsom; the Richmond Royal Horse Show, and Royal Ascot at Ascot Heath; in July the Royal International Horse Show at White City; and in October the Horse of the Year Show at Wembley.

RUGBY FOOTBALL UNION, Whitton Road, Twickenham, Middlesex.

Beginners' courses, initial training and coaching advice can be arranged through County associations. Several major clubs play in or near London and important matches are played at Whitton Road Ground, Twickenham, Middlesex.

SKATING

NATIONAL SKATING ASSOCIATION OF GREAT BRITAIN, Charterhouse, Charterhouse Square, EC1 [253 – 3824].

Tuition for all grades of ice skating is available at all rinks in the London area. Courses are arranged through the CCPR and skates can be hired at all rinks.

The major rinks are Queen's Ice Club, Queensway, W2 [229 – 0172]; The Silver Blades, 386 Streatham High Road, SW16 [769 – 7861] and Richmond Ice Rink, Clevedon Road, East Twickenham [892 – 3646].

You can go roller skating at Alexandra Palace Rink, Wood Green, N22 [883 – 9711].

NATIONAL SKI FEDERATION OF GREAT BRITAIN and SKI CLUB OF GREAT BRITAIN, 118 Eaton Square, SW1 [235 – 8228].

The CCPR and the Ski Club arrange holidays both in Britain and abroad, as do many travel agencies and clubs. Pre-ski training on artificial slopes is available at the National Sports Centre, Crystal Palace, SE19 [778 – 0131]; Simpson (Piccadilly) Ltd, Philbeach Hall, Philbeach Gardens, SW5; and Lillywhites Dry Ski School, Piccadilly Circus, SW1.

SQUASH RACKETS ASSOCIATION, 26 Park Crescent, W1 [636 – 6901].

The growth of squash as a sport is limited by the number of courts available. Courses for beginners, moderate and advanced players are arranged by the CCPR.

SWIMMING AND WATER SPORTS

AMATEUR SWIMMING ASSOCIATION, 64 Cannon Street, EC4 [236 – 4868].

The Association or your local swimming baths can give you details about coaching sessions and swimming tests. There are swimming baths in most boroughs. Here is a brief list. *Indoor*: Buckingham Palace Road, SW1; Caledonian Road, N1; Chelsea Manor Street, SW3; Great Smith Street, SW1; Ironmonger Row, EC1; Marshall Street, W1; Prince of Wales Road, NW5; Porchester Baths, Queensway, W2; Seymour Place, W1; Swiss Cottage, NW1. *Outdoor*: Eltham Park South, SE9; Hampstead Ponds, NW3; Highbury Fields, N5; Highgate Ponds, N6; Kennington Park, SE11; Kenwood Pond, N6; Peckham Rye Park, SE22; Serpentine, Hyde Park, W2; Southwark Park, SE16; Tooting Common, SW17; Victoria Park Lido, E2. The Oasis Pool, Endell Street, WC2 has both indoor and outdoor pools.

ROYAL LIFE SAVING SOCIETY, 14 Devonshire Street, W1 [580 – 5678].

Classes and examinations for RLSS awards are arranged by the Society.

BRITISH WATER SKI FEDERATION, Egham, Surrey.

Residential courses for both elementary and advanced skiers are arranged during the summer.

BRITISH SUB-AQUA CLUB, 160 Great Portland Street, W1 [636 – 5667].

Underwater diving is not a do-it-yourself sport and training is essential. The club's branches will train you if you are over 15 and have fulfilled the club's swimming requirements. Most training is given indoors, but branches organize outdoor expeditions and holidays. Equipment can be hired at teaching sessions, though members are expected to have certain basic equipment, costing about £5.

LAWN TENNIS ASSOCIATION, Queen's Club, Baron's Court, W14 [385 – 2366].

The LTA also has a list of coaches for individuals and small groups.

For a small fee you can become a registered player on the large number of GLC courts and you can then hire a court by the hour at a low cost. Coaching is provided on very reasonable terms. There is a GLC leaflet giving details of courts in their parks which can be obtained from the GLC Parks Department, Cavell House, 2a Charing Cross Road, WC2. Many of the London boroughs also provide tennis courts and details of these can be obtained from the local town hall.

TABLE TENNIS ASSOCIATION, 26 Park Crescent, W1 [580 – 6312].

The Association will give information about coaching and clubs.

AMATEUR VOLLEYBALL ASSOCIATION, c/o Southgate Technical College, High Street, N14.

Courses leading to the coaching award are arranged through the Association and member clubs.

WALKING

Walking in London is often as satisfying as in the country, and at least there are no angry farmers to chase you off their land. There are long traffic-free stretches—across Hampstead Heath to Kenwood, from Queensway to Westminster by way of Kensington Gardens, Hyde Park, Green Park and St James's Park, along the canals, along the Thames, through the acres of Richmond Park. *For organized walks within London see p. 116.*

To enjoy walking in the country you need to know where to go, how to get there, and how to make the most of each area. An organization which will help you to do this is:

RAMBLERS ASSOCIATION, 124 Finchley Road, NW3 [435 – 5481].

The Association exists to protect the interests of all country walkers by working to preserve access to the countryside and footpaths. It organizes special trains and coaches at weekends for parties and provides leaders who know the best routes for walking. Among the outings arranged from London one year were trips to Corfe Castle and the Purbeck Hills, the Pilgrim's Way and the Kent orchards, the New Forest, the cliffs of the Isle of Wight, and Cannock Chase. There are groups of members in various parts of London which arrange their own rambles, London visits and other activities.

Members of the Association receive a bed-and-breakfast and bus-route guide and can borrow ordnance survey maps. Through the Ramblers Association Services Ltd you can arrange individual and group holidays in Britain and abroad.

YOUTH HOSTELS ASSOCIATION, 29 John Adam Street, WC2 [839 – 1722]. *(See p. 183.)*

BRITISH AMATEUR WRESTLING ASSOCIATION, 60 Calabria Road, N5 [226 – 3931].

The Association supplies a list of clubs in the London area.

THE SPORTS CLUB FOR THE BLIND, Grants, Grants Lane, Limpsfield, Oxted, Surrey.

For forty years the Club has organized rowing, tandem-cycling, football, cricket, country rambles, and, during the winter months, weekly social evenings (at St Peter's School, Lower Belgrave Street, SW1) for blind and partially sighted people. Volunteers help with the organization and with the activities. There are seldom sufficient sighted members to allow the sports club to expand to meet all the needs of its blind members.

5

EGGHEAD LONDON

You may have a passionate interest in one particular subject, or you may just be naturally curious about things. Whatever your intellectual idiosyncracies, London's museums, art galleries, public libraries, clubs and associations have so much to offer that you could easily find your leisure hours fuller than your working ones. There are innumerable opportunities to indulge in solitary enjoyment of your particular bent, or join in discussions with people of like mind. So much is happening that the following chapter can give only a brief, selective account of the pleasures in store for the 'egghead' in London with time on his hands. It is not a comprehensive guide but a springboard, designed to give you ideas, and to tell you how you can get in touch with people who share your interests.

LONDON TRANSPORT, 55 Broadway, SW1 [222 – 1234] publish many useful booklets. Of these *Museums and Art Galleries In and Near London* can be had (free) from the Public Relations Officer, 55 Broadway, SW1, or (post free) from The Publicity Office Poster Shop, 280 Old Marylebone Road, NW1. It lists the main museums and art galleries, gives their times of opening and prices of admission, and tells you how to get to them by public transport. *How to Get There* is another useful guide issued by London Transport (5p) and it can be bought at most underground stations. It lists museums, art galleries and places of interest in and around London, tells you how to get to them and how much it costs to go in. This guide covers places on the Green Line bus routes, as far afield as Beaconsfield, Sevenoaks and Hatfield. *Visitor's London* (5p) lists alphabetically places of interest in and near London. A brief description of each place mentioned is given, and there is a separate section on how to get to them.

HER MAJESTY'S STATIONERY OFFICE is the department responsible for publishing Government literature of all kinds. Its publications are on sale in Government bookshops in all the major cities. The address of the London shop is 49 High Holborn, WC1. All the publications in Government bookshops are on sale to the public. They range from copies of Acts of Parliament to leaflets on any number of careers; from ordnance survey maps to guide books, many relating to buildings in London.

THE MINISTRY OF PUBLIC BUILDING AND WORKS. You can apply to the Ministry (CIO Branch), Lambeth Bridge House, Albert Embankment, SE1 [735 – 7611], or at HMSO bookshops or at most museums, for season tickets, 75p, (37½p if you are under 15 or an old-age pensioner) which are valid for one year and which will admit you to all ancient monuments and historic buildings in the Ministry's care. A list of the buildings comes free with your ticket. In London the ticket will admit you to The Banqueting House, Whitehall; The Royal Naval College, Greenwich; Hampton Court; Eltham Palace; The Tower of London; Westminster Abbey and many other places.

For information about museums get hold of *Museums and Galleries in Great Britain and Ireland*, published by Index Publications and obtainable from most bookstalls, 50p. This lists all the London museums and their addresses.

Museums cater for a wide variety of interests, and in many cases offer far more than an opportunity to look at their exhibits. If you find yourself in a museum that specially interests you it is always worth asking if it sponsors any activities in which you can join. Most curators are approachable people, anxious to help those who are genuinely interested.

A poster, *Gallery Guide*, distributed monthly, can be seen on most underground stations. It lists the art exhibitions currently showing at the main museums and galleries in London and gives the nearest station. The poster is published by The Art Exhibitions Bureau, 17 Carlton House Terrace, SW1 [930 – 6844]. For an annual subscription of 50p you can have a miniature version sent to your home address each month.

There are many galleries in London which open only when they have a special exhibition arranged. These include most of the privately owned galleries, and also borough-council-sponsored galleries like The South London Art Gallery, Peckham Road, Camberwell, and the Whitechapel Art Gallery. Details of most temporary exhibitions are advertised in the underground, in the daily press, and on posters displayed locally.

MUSEUMS AND ART GALLERIES

BETHNAL GREEN MUSEUM, Cambridge Heath Road, E2 [980 – 2415]. Admission free, Monday to Saturday, 10 a.m.–6 p.m.; Sunday, 2.30–6.00 p.m.

The building itself rivals its contents in interest. Built in a framework of iron and glass it was originally erected in South Kensington in 1856, where its parent museum, the Victoria and Albert, now stands. It was dismantled and transferred to its present site in 1872 when it was encased in brick. It remains the finest surviving example of the sort of iron and glass construction used by Joseph Paxton.

Special features include local products such as Spitalfields silks, an important collection of English costumes and a collection of dolls and toys for which the museum is specially famous – the earliest toy being a doll's house from Nuremberg dating from the seventeenth century.

BRITISH MUSEUM, Great Russell Street, WC1 [636 – 1555]. Admission free, Monday to Saturday, 10 a.m.–5 p.m.; Sunday, 2.30–6 p.m.

The largest museum of its kind in the world. Its treasures, from all over the world, include the Elgin marbles, the Sutton Hoo ship burial, illuminated manuscripts and a splendid collection of letters and signatures of the famous. You can see the Rosetta Stone, Captain Scott's Diary, and a wonderful collection of old clocks and sundials. The museum also houses the National Library. There are daily guided tours of the galleries, starting from the Entrance Hall at 11.30 a.m. and 3.00 p.m. Ask at the Publications Counter for a plan of the museum. The Department of Ethnography is now at 6 Burlington Gardens, W1.

If you are a student needing to use the museum for your work you can apply for permission to work in one of the students' rooms. Normally speaking admission is only given for advanced research, at postgraduate level, to those who are unable to obtain the books they require from other sources.

BRITISH THEATRE MUSEUM, Leighton House, 12 Holland Park Road, Kensington, W14. Admission free, Tuesday, Thursday, Saturday, 11 a.m.–5 p.m.

A marvellous place to browse if you are a theatre-lover. For the scholar there are the Granville-Barker manuscripts and the contemporary archives of the London Stage Society. There are relics of Garrick, Kean, Kemble, Irving and many other famous actors, and, a nice touch, the piano used during the whole of the record run of *Salad Days*. The curator is glad to help students, research workers and interested members of the public.

BRITISH TRANSPORT MUSEUM, Triangle Place, SW4 [622 – 3241]. Admission 15p, children 10p, Monday to Saturday, 10 a.m.–5.30 p.m.; closed on Sunday.

A fascinating collection of railway carriages, locomotives, buses, trains and relics illustrating the history of public transport in Britain. There are horse-drawn buses and trams, an example of the 'B' type bus, first used in 1910, and a tram dating from 1908, a modified version of which was used until 1952. You can also see Queen Victoria's railway carriage, and the Locomotive, *Mallard,* holder of the world's speed record by steam – 126 m.p.h. – achieved in 1938.

THE COMMONWEALTH INSTITUTE, Kensington High Street, W8 [937 – 8252]. Admission free, Monday to Saturday, 10 a.m.–5.30 p.m.; Sunday, 2.30–6 p.m.

The Institute galleries house permanent exhibits to illustrate life in Commonwealth countries. There is an art gallery in which work by Commonwealth artists is exhibited from time to time. The building has a cinema, an information centre and a reference library (open weekdays, 10 a.m.–6 p.m.) which is available to students, teachers and members of the public on request. The library operates a loan service, details of which can be had from the librarian. Concerts of music or dancing are held at the Institute from time to time, and during the winter months there is a programme of public lectures on Monday evenings from 5.45–

7 p.m. Details of all the Institute's activities can be obtained from the information desk on the ground floor.

COURTAULD INSTITUTE GALLERIES, Courtauld Warburg Building, Woburn Square, WC1 [580 – 1015]. Admission free, Monday to Saturday, 10 a.m.–5 p.m.; Sunday, 2–5 p.m.

A fine collection of paintings belonging to the University of London, including a Botticelli and works by Bellini and Tintoretto. There are English and Dutch portraits, and a wonderful selection of works by the French Impressionists. Cézanne is well represented, and Monet's famous 'Bar at the Folies Bergère' is on view. The galleries are exceptionally well laid out and beautifully lit.

CUMING MUSEUM, Walworth Road, SE17 [703 – 3324]. Admission free, Monday to Saturday, 1.00–5.30 p.m. (Thursday until 7 p.m.; Saturday until 5 p.m.); closed on Sunday.

This museum is concerned mainly with the history and archaeology of Southwark and Lambeth. Among their favourite exhibits are the pump from the Marshalsea debtor's prison, familiar to readers of Dickens, and a 'milk pram' – an old delivery cart complete with churns and measuring-jugs.

CUTTY SARK AND GIPSY MOTH IV, Greenwich Pier, SE10 [858 – 3445]. Cutty Sark 10p, Children 5p; Gipsy Moth IV 7½p, Children 2½p. Monday to Saturday, 11 a.m.–5 p.m.; Sunday, 2.30–5 p.m.; open till 6 p.m. in the summer.

Cutty Sark is the last of the great Clipper ships and is preserved as a museum to show what life was like on such a ship. There is a splendid collection of figureheads. *Gipsy Moth IV* is the ship in which Sir Francis Chichester sailed single-handed round the world.

DICKENS HOUSE, 48 Doughty Street, WC1 [405 – 2127]. Admission 15p, students 10p, children 5p. Monday to Saturday, 10 a.m.–5 p.m.; closed on Sunday and Bank Holidays.

Dickens lived here from 1837 to 1839. The house contains portraits, letters, illustrations, relics, and the most complete library of books by and connected with Dickens that exists. Research facilities for students can be provided by appointment.

DULWICH COLLEGE PICTURE GALLERY, College Road, SE21 [693 – 3737]. Admission free, Tuesday to Saturday, May to August, 10 a.m.–6 p.m.; 1 September to 15 October, 10 a.m.–5 p.m.; 16 March to 30 April, 10 a.m.–5 p.m.; 16 October to 15 March, 10 a.m.–4 p.m.; Sunday, May to August, 2 p.m.–6 p.m.; Sunday, April and September, 2 p.m.–5 p.m.; closed on Mondays.

Distinguished not only for its collection but because it was London's first public art gallery. Paintings include work by English, French and Dutch painters.

FENTON HOUSE, Hampstead Grove, NW3 [435 – 3471]. Adults 20p, children 10p, gardens only 7½p. Monday, Wednesday, Thursday, Friday, Saturday, 11 a.m.–5 p.m.; Sunday, 2–5 p.m.; closed on Tuesdays.

Fenton House was bequeathed to the National Trust in 1952 by Lady Binning, together with her fine collection of predominantly eighteenth-century furniture, pottery and porcelain. The Trust decided that Fenton House would make an ideal home for a collection of early keyboard instruments left to it in 1938. Harpsichord students may ask the curator for permission to play the harpsichords in this collection.

GEFFRYE MUSEUM, Kingsland Road, E2 [739 – 8368]. Admission free, Tuesday to Saturday, 10 a.m.–5 p.m.; Sunday, 2–5 p.m.; closed Mondays.

The museum was originally the Ironmongers' Almshouses. Now famous for its collection of furniture and woodwork from Elizabethan times to the present day, displayed room by room. Many exhibits have been rescued from demolished London houses. There are children's workrooms and a lecture room–exhibition hall. A reference library of books on furniture and social history is available to students and visitors alike.

GEOLOGICAL MUSEUM, Exhibition Road, SW7 [589 – 9441]. Admission free, Monday to Saturday, 10 a.m.–6 p.m.; Sunday, 2.30–6 p.m.; Library, Monday–Saturday, 10 a.m.–6 p.m.

The Museum houses exhibits illustrating the geology of Great Britain, economic geology and geological processes such as volcanicity, metamorphism, marine action, glaciation, etc. It has a unique collection of rare and beautiful gemstones and a spectacular collection of British minerals. An exhibit on the geography and geology of the moon, which outlines the progress in lunar exploration is on view at the time of writing.

The Reference Library of literature, maps and photographs is open free to the public.

On Tuesday, Wednesday, Thursday and Saturday afternoons illustrated lectures, demonstrations or film showings are held in the Museum – subjects include volcanoes, mineral exploration, Ice Ages and the moon. Programme free on request.

GUILDHALL LIBRARY AND ART GALLERY, Guildhall, King Street, EC2 [606 – 3030]. Admission free, Monday to Saturday, 9.30 a.m.–5 p.m.; Art Gallery, 10 a.m.–5 p.m.

Situated in the precincts of Guildhall, the Library is a general reference library with extensive collections of manuscripts and prints relating to London.

The Art Gallery holds exhibitions of the following types: selections from its permanent collection, loan exhibitions of Old Masters, art exhibitions sponsored by the City, annual exhibitions of approved Art Societies. The Gallery is closed between exhibitions, which are held each month and last about three weeks.

GUILDHALL MUSEUM, Gillett House, Bassishaw Highwalk, Off London Wall [606 – 3030]. Admission free, Monday to Saturday, 10 a.m.–5 p.m.

The exhibition in the museum is divided into two parts: Roman antiquities, including the Head of Mithras and other finds from the Temple of Mithras unearthed in the City in 1954; and medieval and later antiquities. There is also a leathercraft museum showing examples of leatherwork from Roman times to the present day.

GUNNERSBURY PARK MUSEUM, Gunnersbury Park, W3 [992 – 2247/8]. Admission free, April to September, Monday to Friday, 2–5 p.m.; and Saturday, Sunday, 2–6 p.m.; October to March, daily, 2–4 p.m.

Formerly a Rothschild family home, this interesting museum of local history has exhibits from the Stone Age to modern times, designed to illustrate and explain the history, life and development of the locality. For archaeologists there is material from Northolt Manor, and acquisitions not on show can be seen by appointment. If you are interested in social history there are, among other things, two coaches used by the Rothschild family, examples of nineteenth- and twentieth-century costume, and Victorian and Edwardian laundry equipment.

HAYWARD GALLERY, South Bank, SE1 [928 – 3144]. Monday, Wednesday, Friday, Saturday, 10 a.m.–6 p.m.; Tuesday, Thursday, 10 a.m.–8 p.m.; Sunday, 12 noon–6 p.m.

This gallery is London's temporary exhibition centre, featuring art exhibitions of all periods organized by the Arts Council of Great Britain. When an exhibition is on show, dates and prices of admission are widely advertised in underground stations and in the press.

HOGARTH'S HOUSE, Hogarth Lane, Chiswick, W4 [994 – 6757]. Admission 5p, children 3p, Monday to Saturday, 11 a.m.– 6 p.m.; Sunday, 2–6 p.m.; October to April, closes 4 p.m.

It seems hard to believe now, as you follow the traffic along the M4, that this was Hogarth's country house. He lived in it off and on for over fifteen years. The house contains a fine collection of drawings and engravings, together with some relics of his life.

HORNIMAN MUSEUM, London Road, SE23, [699 – 2339]. Admission free, Monday to Saturday, 10.30 a.m.–6 p.m.; Sunday, 2–6 p.m.

A fascinating collection illustrating man and his environment. Examples of simple tools, primitive art, including masks, fetishes, and religious and magical objects. There is a zoology section (with an aquarium) dealing with classification, evolution, animal locomotion and defence. Another feature is a large collection of musical instruments. The library has 40,000 books on anthropology and zoology. There is a programme of lectures and concerts for which details can be obtained from the museum.

IMPERIAL WAR MUSEUM, Lambeth Road, SE1 [735 – 8922]. Admission free, Monday to Saturday, 10 a.m.–6 p.m.; Sunday, 2–6 p.m.; Reference Library, Tuesday to Friday, 10 a.m.–5 p.m.

As well as its vast collection of military objects from two world wars, the Imperial War Museum owns about three million classified photographs and thousands of miles of film covering war, diplomacy and social life since 1914. Students and other groups can arrange to see selections from this unique material. Unexpectedly, perhaps, the Imperial War Museum also houses one of the biggest art collections in Britain, some 9,000 wartime paintings by leading artists including Piper, Nash and Ardizzone. The library has a large collection of printed and manuscript material, which is held in reserve; it can be seen by appointment. Films from the museum's archives are normally shown at noon (Monday to Friday), 2.45 p.m. and 4 p.m. (Sunday).

INSTITUTE OF CONTEMPORARY ARTS, Nash House, The Mall, SW1 [839 – 5344]. Hours and prices of admission to the gallery vary according to what is showing, so ring up or check with a gallery guide before you go along.

The aim of the Institute, founded in 1947 by the late Sir Herbert Read, is to provide a platform for new developments in all the arts. Membership of the ICA entitles you to attend (at half-price) or take part in all the activities sponsored by the Institute, and to receive the monthly calendar, *Eventsheet*. The films shown in the Institute's cinema are open to members only. Regular concerts of modern classical music, pop and jazz are held, and there are readings, discussions and lectures. You can be a standard member (£2 a year) or a full member (£5 a year). Full members are admitted free (with one free guest) to all exhibitions, and receive invitations to opening parties. Standard members are admitted to exhibitions at half-price. (*See p. 22.*)

THE JEWISH MUSEUM, Woburn House, Upper Woburn Place, WC1 [387 – 3081]. Admission free, Monday to Thursday, 2.30–5 p.m.; Friday and Sunday, 10 a.m.–1 p.m.; closed on Saturdays, Jewish Holy Days and Bank Holidays.

A collection of items in wood, pottery, silver, ivory and textiles illustrating the religious life of the Jews, both public and domestic. Conducted tours for parties can be arranged by appointment.

DR JOHNSON'S HOUSE, 17 Gough Square, EC4 [353 – 3745]. Admission 10p, students and children 5p, Monday to Saturday (May to September), 10.30 a.m.–5 p.m.; October to April, 10.30 a.m.–4.30 p.m.; closed on Sunday.

Apart from the fact that this is a lovely Queen Anne House, it is well worth a visit because it was here that Dr Johnson compiled his famous Dictionary. There is still an atmosphere of learning in the air, and you can see portraits and relics of Dr Johnson and his friends, as well as first editions of his books.

KEATS HOUSE, Keats Grove, NW3 [435 – 2062]. Admission

free, Monday to Saturday (house), 10 a.m.–6 p.m.; Monday to Friday (library), 9 a.m.–7 p.m.; Saturday, 9.30 a.m.–5 p.m.

In the house are relics of Keats, books and annotated letters. The next-door public library houses the Keats Memorial Library containing early editions of Keats and his contemporaries.

KENWOOD HOUSE, Hampstead Lane, NW3 [348 – 1286]. Admission free, except Saturday and Monday, when admission for adults is 15p and children 5p.

The paintings on view are part of the collection acquired by the first Lord Iveagh, who bequeathed the house and grounds to the nation in 1927. Look out especially for fine examples of the work of Rembrandt, Vermeer, Gainsborough and Reynolds.

The house is set in a fine park, open to the public, and a very good place for walks and picnics. Kenwood is one of the parks in which open-air evening concerts sponsored by the GLC are given in summer. Watch park notice-boards for dates and times and remember they may be cancelled if it is wet.

LEIGHTON HOUSE MUSEUM AND ART GALLERY, 12 Holland Park Road, W14 [937 – 9916]. Admission free, Monday to Saturday, 11 a.m.–5 p.m.; Monday to Friday, 11 a.m.–6 p.m. during temporary exhibitions.

Formerly the house of Lord Leighton, painter and art collector. There is a fine hall, designed in the Persian manner and tiled with fourteenth- to sixteenth-century tiles brought back from the Middle East by Lord Leighton. Paintings by Lord Leighton and other Kensington artists are on permanent exhibition, together with pottery and tiles by William de Morgan. An exhibition of High Victorian Art, which includes furniture by nineteenth-century designers and paintings by Burne-Jones, Watts, Alma Tadema, Millais and other contemporary artists, is a permanent feature. Temporary exhibitions are also mounted.

Courses of lectures covering the fine and applied arts are held in the evenings from October to December and January to March. The studio on the first floor can be hired for concerts and lectures.

THE LONDON MUSEUM AND THE STATE APARTMENTS OF KENSINGTON PALACE, Kensington Palace, W8 [937 – 9816]. Admission free, Monday to Saturday, 10 a.m.–6 p.m.; Sunday, 2–6 p.m.; October to February the museum closes at 4 p.m.

The museum's exhibition illustrates the history and social life of London from its beginnings, and includes maps and paintings, costume, pottery and porcelain, metalwork, glasswork and jewellery. Only a part of the collection is on view at any one time, but students may apply to the Director to see stored material.

NATIONAL GALLERY, Trafalgar Square, WC2 [930 – 7618]. Admission free, Monday to Saturday, 10 a.m.–6 p.m.; Sunday, 2–6 p.m.; from June to September, open until 9 p.m. on Tuesday and Thursday.

The gallery houses one of the finest collections of paintings in the world, representing all the famous European schools of art from the thirteenth to the nineteenth centuries. Free lectures are given four times a week. For times and subjects see notices at the gallery.

NATIONAL MARITIME MUSEUM, Romney Road, Greenwich, SE10 [858 – 4422]. Admission free, Monday to Saturday, 10 a.m.–6 p.m.; Sunday, 2.30–6 p.m.

A survey of naval history, including the Merchant Navy and Fishing Fleet, from Tudor times to the present day. There is an especially fine display of material connected with Nelson. The museum's collection of sea-scapes and naval pictures is un-matched. The Print Room has some 350,000 items, most of which are kept in the students' room, where they are available for the use of students by appointment. The library reading-room is also available for study by appointment.

The National Maritime Museum stands nearby the river Thames at Greenwich. Rising behind it is Greenwich Park, a place for walks, picnics, fine views and (incidentally) great for tobogganing in the winter. At the top of the hill is the old Royal Observatory, housed in Flamstead House, a lovely house built by Wren in 1675 for the Reverend John Flamstead, the first Astronomer Royal. The Octagon Room has been kept as it was in his day, and across the courtyard runs the Greenwich Meridian, agreed internationally in 1884 to be the Prime Meridian of the world. The rooms now open to the public are furnished with period furniture, and house a display of sand-glasses and sun-dials, navigational and astronomical instruments, and tele-scopes of considerable interest. The South Building contains a planetarium in which demonstrations are given to schools and the public.

NATIONAL PORTRAIT GALLERY, 2 St Martin's Place, Trafalgar Square, WC2 [930 – 8511]. Admission free, Monday to Friday, 10 a.m.–5 p.m.; Saturday, 10 a.m.–6 p.m.; Sunday, 2–6 p.m.

Here there are portraits of people from Tudor times to the present day, who have made a mark in the nation's history in politics, literature, science, music and other walks of life.

NATIONAL POSTAL MUSEUM, King Edward Building, King Edward Street, EC1 [432 – 3851]. Admission free, Monday to Friday, 10 a.m.–4.30 p.m.; Saturday, 10 a.m.–4 p.m.; closed on Sunday.

This is a 'must' for anyone interested in postage stamps and their role in the economic and social life of the country since 1840. The finest collection in the world of stamps of Great Britain is on display, a collection particularly strong in unique unissued and proof material. The British stamps are supplemented by an almost complete collection of all the stamps issued by every postal administration in the world since 1878 (and many earlier issues). Lectures and film shows on philatelic and related subjects are given and there is a specialized reference library. As far as possible the staff are ready to give help, advice and information to visitors.

NATURAL HISTORY MUSEUM, Cromwell Road, SW7 [589 – 6323]. Admission free, Monday to Saturday, 10 a.m.–6 p.m.; Sunday, 2.30–6 p.m.

The galleries, which are vast in scope and layout, contain large selections of specimens of animals and plants, extinct as well as existing, the rocks and minerals which make up the earth's crust, and special exhibits illustrating evolution and other biological topics. There is also a year-round programme of afternoon public lectures (weekdays 3 p.m.) illustrating various aspects of natural history. The subjects dealt with include wildlife in Britain, domestic animals, animals as pets, African game, British wild flowers, London's wildlife, natural selection, and so on. Many of the lectures are illustrated with films. A list is available from the Museum.

PHOTOGRAPHERS' GALLERY, 8 Great Newport Street, WC2 [836 – 7860]. Admission 20p, 10p for students. Tuesday to Saturday 11 a.m.–7 p.m.; Sunday 12–6 p.m. Closed on Monday.

The only gallery in London devoted entirely to photographic exhibitions. The work on show is changed each month.

PIANO AND MUSICAL MUSEUM, 368 High Street, Brentford, Middlesex [560 – 8108]. Donation for entry 20p, March to November, Thursday, Saturday and Sunday, 2.30–6 p.m. Otherwise closed.

For those interested in 'automatic, old and odd musical instruments' a trip to Brentford High Street (not far from Kew) is well worthwhile. Here, in an unexpected gothic setting you will find delicate, automatically played musical instruments. The Museum's director organizes explanatory tours lasting an hour or more, during which demonstrations are given and you can hear, amongst other things, an Orchestrion – a complete orchestra, and a Violona-Virtuoso – a violin played automatically with piano accompaniment. The museum's collection includes nickelodions, street organs, musical boxes and a piano with two vertical keyboards.

THE PUBLIC RECORD OFFICE MUSEUM, Chancery Lane, WC2 [405 – 0741]. Admission free, Monday to Friday, 1–4 p.m.

The museum itself is of considerable interest, since it was built on the site of the Chapel of the House of the Converts, founded by Henry III in 1232 to receive Jews into the Christian faith. Its most famous possession is the Domesday Book, and you can also see the Papal Bull confirming to Henry VIII the title of *Fidei Defensor*, Wellington's dispatch from Waterloo, and the log of the Victory at Trafalgar.

THE QUEEN'S GALLERY, Buckingham Palace Road, SW1. Admission 15p, Tuesday to Saturday, 11 a.m.–5 p.m.; Sunday, 2–5 p.m.; closed on Monday.

The Queen's Gallery is in Buckingham Palace. A small selection of the vast art collection belonging to The Royal Collection is on display. The selection is changed every now and then, and during the time that the new exhibition is being mounted the gallery is closed.

ROYAL ACADEMY, Burlington House, Piccadilly, W1 [734 –

9052]. Admission 40p, Monday to Saturday, 10 a.m.–6 p.m.; Sunday, 2–6 p.m.

There is an annual Summer Exhibition of the work of living artists. At other times of the year loan exhibitions of works by a single artist, or artists from a particular country, or of a certain school or group are mounted. Prices of admission vary for these exhibitions.

THE ROYAL BOTANIC GARDENS KEW, Kew, Surrey [940 – 1171]. Admission 1p, Gardens, 10 a.m.–4 p.m. in winter, 8 p.m. in summer; Houses, 1–4.50 p.m., weekdays, 5.50 p.m. Sunday.

Stretching along the Thames at Kew, the gardens are a lovely place to go to, whether you want to relax on the lawns, or study some of the 25,000 or more plants that grow there. Research is the keynote of Kew, and one of the chief tasks of the staff is the identification and classification of specimens. The Herbarium, and the extensive library, are not open to the public, but may be used by *bona fide* researchers. One of the nicest places in the gardens is the Marianne North Gallery, which houses the paintings of this tireless Victorian botanist, who travelled across the world painting plants in their natural settings.

Other buildings of special interest are Sir William Chambers's famous Pagoda and Orangery, the Palm House, Kew Palace, and the charming Queen's Cottage, built in the second half of the eighteenth century and surrounded by natural woodland.

ROYAL COLLEGE OF MUSIC, Prince Consort Road, SW7 [589 – 3643]. Admission free, Monday and Wednesday, 10.30 a.m. – 4.30 p.m. during college term, by previous appointment with the curator.

A general collection of nearly four hundred keyboard, wind and string instruments, mostly European, but there are some folk instruments from the Near East, India, Africa, China and Japan.

THE SCIENCE MUSEUM, South Kensington, SW7 [589 – 6371]. Admission free, Monday to Saturday, 10 a.m.–6 p.m.; Sunday, 2.30–6 p.m.

The museum's extensive galleries are devoted to all branches of science, and many of the exhibits include working models which can be operated by visitors. Illustrated lectures are usually given on Tuesdays, Thursdays and Saturdays. The subjects covered are normally linked to the collections in the museum, for example, the railway collection, the map-making and survey collection, the chemistry collection, and so on. A programme of the month's lectures and films is available free on request.

The library is open free to the public from 10 a.m. to 5.30 p.m. on weekdays, and the museum produces many pamphlets and booklets, a list of which is available.

THE SERPENTINE GALLERY, West Carriageway, Kensington Gardens, W8. Admission free, open daily, May to September, 11 a.m.–8 p.m.; October, closes at 6.30 p.m.

Some time ago the neo-palladian tea-house near the Serpentine Bridge in Kensington Gardens, well known to generations of Londoners, was closed. Now the building has become an art gallery, opened by the Arts Council of Great Britain specially to provide a gallery in which the work of young artists can be shown. When the work of conversion began the Arts Council realized they had been offered an ideal building. Its glass domes and french windows provide excellent lighting, and its situation in the park gives the gallery, with its four exhibition spaces, the informal, leisure-time atmosphere that is wanted.

Posters giving details of current exhibitions are displayed in the park, and advertised in the press.

SIR JOHN SOANE'S MUSEUM, 13 Lincoln's Inn Fields, WC2 [405 – 2107]. Admission free, Tuesday to Saturday, 10 a.m.–5 p.m.; closed on Sunday and Monday; closed during August.

A private collection of antiquities and works of art gathered by Sir John Soane. The collection is still exactly as he arranged it before his death, in the house he built for himself. It includes Hogarth's *Rake's Progress* and works by Turner and Canaletto. There are guided lecture-tours on Saturday afternoon at 2.30 p.m.

THE TATE GALLERY, Millbank, SW1 [828 – 1212]. Admission free, Monday to Saturday, 10 a.m.–6 p.m.; Sunday, 2–6 p.m.

The Tate Gallery houses two main collections: British painting up to 1900, and modern painting and sculpture, both British and foreign, including examples of work by contemporary artists. Special exhibitions to which admission is charged are held regularly.

Free guide lectures are given on Tuesday at 1 p.m., Thursday at 1 p.m. and 3 p.m., and Saturday at 3 p.m. Look out especially for the collection of paintings by Turner and Constable, Blake and the Pre-Raphaelites.

VICTORIA AND ALBERT MUSEUM, South Kensington, SW7 [589 – 6371]. Admission free, Monday to Saturday, 10 a.m.–6 p.m.; Sunday, 2.30–6 p.m.

A good guide to this museum of fine art is on sale for 15p at the bookstall. The best advice that can be given to anyone who wants to make use of the numerous facilities offered by this lively and enterprising museum is to go and look at the pamphlets and booklets giving up-to-date information of times of lectures and subjects. The Public Relations and Enquiry Office is in Room 10. Special exhibitions are mounted from time to time for which an admission fee is occasionally charged. The museum houses, incidentally, the largest art library in the world.

Afternoon and evening lectures are given on such subjects as English art, taste in the nineteenth century, the great patrons, introduction to antiques. The museum also arranges films and lectures specially for young people. Subjects vary, and leaflets can be sent on application. One year, for example, there were films on Picasso and the ballet, and a lecture on singing and musical instruments, illustrated with songs. The museum staff can arrange, without charge, to give a lecture on any subject within the museum's scope, provided that the request is made well in advance, and an audience of interested people is guaranteed.

The museum has a season of chamber-music concerts each summer, normally on Sunday evenings. For details of programmes and prices of admission ask at the museum. The concerts are well attended, and if you are interested it is as well to apply early for tickets, at the usual agencies. Unreserved tickets are on sale at the Museum on concert nights only.

THE WALLACE COLLECTION, Hertford House, Manchester Square, W1 [935 – 0687]. Admission free, Monday to Saturday, 10 a.m.–5 p.m.; Sunday, 2–5 p.m.

An outstanding collection of works of art of all kinds bequeathed to the nation by Lady Wallace in 1897, and still displayed in the house of its founders. There are important pictures by artists of all European Schools, including Titian, Rubens, Van Dyck, Rembrandt, Hals, Velazquez, Murillo, Reynolds, Gainsborough, and Delacroix; unrivalled representation of the arts of France in the eighteenth century, including paintings (Watteau, Boucher, Fragonard especially), sculpture, goldsmith's work, and Sèvres porcelain; and also a valuable collection of majolica, European and Oriental arms and armour.

WELLCOME FOUNDATION BUILDING, 183 Euston Road, NW1 [387 – 4477]. Admission free, Monday to Friday, 10 a.m.–5 p.m.; Saturday, 9.30 a.m.–4.30 p.m.; closed on Sunday.

The museum and library of the Wellcome Institute of the History of Medicine, a collection of original material, books and manuscripts relating to the history of medicine, surgery and allied sciences from very early times, is housed here. Early pharmacies have been reconstructed with contemporary equipment.

WELLINGTON MUSEUM, Apsley House, 149 Piccadilly, W1 [499 – 5676]. Admission 5p, children 2½p. Monday to Saturday, 10 a.m.–6 p.m.; Sunday, 2.30–6 p.m.

Here are relics of the first Duke of Wellington, whose house this was, including fine paintings, portraits, swords, silver plate, porcelain and other works of art. This is the first house after Hyde Park Corner and was once known as Number One, London.

LIBRARIES

Public Libraries

London's public libraries are much more than collections of books for borrowing. True, their principal function is to provide books for information, study and leisure, but they are also a wonderful source of neighbourhood information. Again and again in this book you will come across some such sentence as 'ask at your local public library'. This gives the key to the part the library plays in the life of the locality. The public libraries of London are borough services and the quality of the service depends, to some extent, on the attitude of the borough council. Similarly the full range of services found in a central library cannot be found in every small neighbourhood branch. Even if the library you go to regularly can't give you the address of a particular club or society, or provide information about the local adult education institute, it can direct you to a central library which will almost certainly be able to help.

Many libraries provide national and local newspapers, periodicals and journals, both current issues and back numbers. The larger libraries provide tables and chairs for those using reference books and some, including Hornsey, West Norwood, Swiss Cottage and Holborn have study booths which you can book in advance.

Records can be borrowed in all London boroughs (except one). The collections are usually in central or main libraries, and, apart from classical discs, may include jazz, pop, speech, and languages.

To brighten your room pictures can be borrowed from some libraries: Camden will lend original paintings and prints, Greenwich lends original prints, Hackney, Haringey and Lewisham, among others, lend reproductions, Westminster has a Fine Arts Library which has books, periodicals and reproductions as well as a collection of 2 ins. × 2 ins. colour transparencies available for use in the library.

Some boroughs have acquired special collections, for example Westminster's central reference library in St Martin's Street, WC2 has over six hundred volumes about and by William Blake; at Camden's Heath branch library in Keats Grove, NW3 there is a collection of books about John Keats and his contemporaries. All boroughs have collections of historical material about the locality: books, pamphlets, posters, newspaper cuttings, documents, photographs, and so on.

You will find that libraries have always been generous in cooperating with each other – all to the ultimate benefit of the library user who can, for example, use his library ticket at *any* of London's libraries. The London Special Collection scheme, now over twenty years old, provides for the purchase of all new British books and the preservation of older books so that comprehensive collections are available in London. For instance, Westminster specializes in music, Islington in photography,

Hammersmith in law and public administration, Camden in psychology and philosophy, Kensington in biography, and Southwark in general history and the ancient world. The list is endless. The collections do not include standard text books (this is not generally regarded as the public libraries' function in any field) but rather provide wide and detailed background reading. Books from these collections can be borrowed through your local library which, through regional, national and sometimes international cooperative machinery, can obtain books not in stock locally from other libraries.

Most libraries issue a pamphlet guide to membership, hours of opening and services – get one from your local library.

Other Libraries

THE LONDON LIBRARY, 14 St James's Square, SW1 [930 – 7705]. Annual subscription £21, Monday to Saturday, 9.30 a.m.–5.30 p.m., (Thursday, open till 7.30 p.m.); closed on Sunday.

The London Library has up to a million books and periodicals in its possession. The collection includes fiction in English and most European languages, and non-fiction excluding science, law and medicine. Up to ten books can be borrowed at a time (fifteen if you live outside London), and the initial loan period is two months. Books can be sent by post – postage both ways is chargeable to the borrower.

CLUBS AND ASSOCIATIONS

Art and Architecture

GREATER LONDON ARTS ASSOCIATION, 27 Southampton Street, WC2 [836 – 5225].

The Association is one of a number of regional arts associations supported by the Arts Council of Great Britain, the local authorities and commercial and private patrons. It aims to encourage the practice and appreciation of professional and amateur arts among those living in the thirty-two London boroughs. It is also the co-ordinating body for the thirty or so local arts councils that flourish all over London. The councils themselves act mainly as co-ordinating centres for the various cultural activities and arts societies in their boroughs. You can get the address of your local arts council from Southampton Street or the public library. The arts councils sponsor and help to organize such things as drama festivals, music festivals, exhibitions of paintings, walks of architectural and historic interest and poetry readings. Summer schools are organized by the Association and in 1970 there was an Arts Appreciation cruise round the Mediterranean coast.

Many of the activities sponsored by local Associations depend on voluntary help – indeed the Association's policy is just as much aimed at encouraging people to make their own entertainment as it is at helping professionals by sponsorship.

The Association publishes a *Newsletter* (monthly) obtainable from the above address. The annual subscription is 50p or £1 for Associate Membership, which includes a subscription to the *Newsletter* and Artsmail.

Art Societies

ARTSMAIL, 92 Brompton Road, SW3 [584 – 5228].

Artsmail is a mailing service organized under the auspices of the Greater London Arts Council designed to circulate a variety of information on entertainment and leisure activities.

Subscribers and their interests are coded on a computer-based file. Another file holds dates and details of activities. The computer matches these two and prints out a personal newsletter to each subscriber giving details of the events which interest him. Leaflets, booking forms and other promotional material are also sent out.

The list covers music (orchestral, guitar recitals, brass band, folk, jazz, pop, chamber, etc.), theatre (including mime, variety, puppetry and circus), visual arts (including architecture, metalwork, costume, antiques, crafts), dance, films, literature, modern and experimental arts, and activities for children. The list is further sub-divided so that you can be sent material on these subjects related to particular periods.

Related information which is available comes under the headings of festivals, group bookings, records, tapes and books.

You subscribe at different rates depending on how many interests you wish to receive information on.

Many local art societies meet in London, and if you are interested in painting, either as an artist or because you like looking at pictures, membership of an art group would help you to meet other people who share your interest.

ART SOCIETY OF PADDINGTON, Honorary Secretary, Miss E. Camp, 27 Moorhouse Road, W2 is fairly representative of art societies in general. Membership is open to practising artists and those interested in art, in Paddington and the adjoining boroughs. The Society holds several exhibitions for members each year, and has an annual film show of Arts Council art films. They have occasional wine parties, and meet from time to time to criticise members' work. The annual subscription is £1.

Cultural Institutes

Many foreign countries have cultural institutes in London, which you can join by paying an annual subscription. Most of them have excellent libraries of books in their own language, and their activities include language classes, lectures, film shows and visits to theatres and places of interest. Addresses and telephone numbers can be found in the telephone directory or, if you prefer, you can get in touch with the appropriate embassy and ask for details from the Cultural Attaché.

Amenity Societies

Amenity societies operate in various ways, and for different specific reasons, but the main aim of most of them is to keep a watchful eye on the activities of the re-developers. They fall into two main groups: district societies and period societies. Your local public library will tell you if there is a society in your district, and if so, whom to get in touch with for details of how to join.

CIVIC TRUST, 18 Carlton House Terrace, SW1 [930 – 0914].

The Civic Trust was founded in 1957 with the aim of improving the appearance of town and country. It is a recognized charity, supported by voluntary contributions.

The Trust has initiated hundreds of schemes to brighten and tidy up drab streets, stimulated voluntary action to remove eyesores which spoil the town and the countryside, and has promoted new techniques for moving semi-mature trees as part of a wider campaign to plant more trees. By conferences, projects and reports it focuses attention on major issues in town planning and architecture. The Trust was closely associated with the drafting of the Civic Amenities Act, 1967, and now gives support and advice to over 700 local civic and amenity societies. The Trust, or your public library, will give you the address of your local amenity society.

THE GEORGIAN GROUP, 12 Chester Square, SW1 [235 – 3081] is a similar society whose interests range far beyond London, as do those of the SOCIETY FOR THE PROTECTION OF ANCIENT BUILDINGS, 55 Great Ormond Street, WC1 [405 – 2646] and the ANCIENT MONUMENTS SOCIETY, whose secretary lives at 11 Alexander Street, W2.

All these societies need your money and welcome your support. If you are really interested in preserving what is good in your environment then you could find membership worthwhile in the long run. They are not in any sense clubs, however, and do not arrange regular programmes of meetings or social events.

THE KENSINGTON SOCIETY, Mrs Christiansen, 18 Kensington Square, W8 [937 – 0931] is an active local group which not only watches over the fate of houses in Kensington scheduled for demolition, but also holds meetings from time to time, and organizes occasional walks in the district.

THE PADDINGTON SOCIETY, Honorary Secretary, Mrs Louis Hettena, 30 Westbourne Park Villas, W2 [229 – 3281].

The Society is both an historical and an amenity society and is one of the six main preservation societies in Westminster recognized by the Westminster City Council for the purposes of planning consultation. Its aim is to maintain and, where necessary, stimulate a feeling for the long history of the old Borough of

Paddington, to research into the past and to obtain support for its efforts to save areas of architectural and historic interest from unwise development. New members are welcome, so are offers of help and interest in the Society's many activities.

It meets for lectures, discussions and film shows on the last Friday of each month, from September to June, details of which appear in the local press and on posters throughout the area. Outings to places of interest are arranged. The Society's annual programme can be had from the Honorary Secretary (enclose a stamped addressed envelope).

PLANNING FORUM, annual subscription 75p, is an independent offshoot of the above Association. It is a discussion group which meets monthly to talk over planning subjects of topical interest. During the summer the group goes on guided visits to places of planning interest in and around London.

TOWN AND COUNTRY PLANNING ASSOCIATION, 28 King Street, Covent Garden, WC2 [836 – 5006/7]. Annual Subscription £5, students £2.

If you are interested in what is happening to your environment, either locally or nationally, membership of the Town and Country Planning Association keeps you in touch, especially locally, with planning proposals. The Association welcomes support from individual members for its policy of encouraging good planning. Members receive the monthly journal and notices of all conferences, study tours and meetings.

THE VICTORIAN SOCIETY, 12 Magnolia Wharf, Strand-on-the-Green, W8 [994 – 1510] is active all over the country in trying to forestall the destruction of Victorian buildings of architectural or historic interest. The London branch arranges meetings and walks.

Historical and Archaeological

THE HISTORICAL ASSOCIATION, 59a Kennington Park Road, SE11 [735 – 3901]. Annual membership fee, £1 or £1·75 with *History*; 50p less for those of 18 or under.

The aims of the Association are to advance the study and teaching of history at all levels, and to increase public interest in all aspects of the subject. It publishes the periodical *History*, and other bulletins and pamphlets, and its local branches arrange meetings and discussions. The Association also runs a week-long vacation school annually, primarily intended for those really interested in history and its teaching.

THE CAMDEN HISTORY SOCIETY, St Pancras Library, 100 Euston Road, London NW1 [586 – 0061]. Annual subscription £1, joint membership for husband and wife £1·50, students and pensioners 50p.

Founded to encourage an interest in local history, the Society arranges research projects, lectures, visits to places of local interest, and publishes a magazine. To find out more, ring St Pancras Library and ask to speak to the Secretary, Mr G. F. Gregory, or write to him there.

History Societies, usually founded by a group of enthusiasts to research into local history and record findings, can be found in many other boroughs. The Marylebone History Society, for example, is a well-known and active group. Your local library will put you in touch with the secretary of the group in your area.

ARCHITECTURAL AND HISTORICAL WALKS, International House, 33 Shaftesbury Avenue, W1 [437 – 9167].

For those who want to know more about some of London's most famous places a series of lectures followed by visits is given on Saturdays at International House throughout the year. Parties are limited to twenty, so it is worthwhile ringing the above number to book a place in advance. The lectures begin at 10.30 a.m. They are followed by the walk, and the total time involved is about three and a half hours. Places visited on different Saturdays include the Tower of London, a tour of Medieval London, the City churches, Roman London, St Paul's Cathedral and Fleet Street. The fee for each session is 40p.

COUNCIL FOR BRITISH ARCHAEOLOGY, 8 St Andrew's Place, Regent's Park, NW1 [486 – 1527].

The Council is the coordinating body for British Archaeological Societies. From March to September it issues a monthly *Calendar of Excavations* currently being carried out, together with information about the kind of voluntary help that is welcomed by the organizers of each dig. Annual subscription to the

Calendar is 50p, and it can be obtained from the Secretary. Voluntary help is not normally accepted from those under the age of 16. On some digs help is only sought from those who have had previous experience, but don't be put off by this, because there are organizers who are glad of help from the inexperienced, and who feel that if you are interested and want to learn, that makes up for lack of experience.

ROYAL ARCHAEOLOGICAL INSTITUTE, Assistant Secretary, Mrs H. Saunders, 9 Somerset Road, New Barnet, Hertfordshire.

The Institute is open to amateur and professional archaeologists but membership is by election. A *Journal* is published annually. The Institute's activities include a summer meeting lasting a week, based on a centre outside London, one-day visits to places of interest in the spring and autumn, and lectures on subjects of archaeological or historical and architectural interest. For further details write to the Assistant Secretary at the above address.

CITY OF LONDON ARCHAEOLOGICAL SOCIETY, c/o The Guildhall Museum, EC2 [606 – 3030].

The Society is involved with excavations within the City of London. It has a waiting list of helpers and does not normally accept offers of help in excavation from those who have had no previous experience. It arranges lectures and courses of study, however, for its members.

SOUTHWARK AND LAMBETH ARCHAEOLOGICAL SOCIETY. Inquiries to: The Cuming Museum, Walworth Road, SE17 [703 – 3324]. Annual subscription £1, children under 16 50p.

The primary function of the Society is to conduct excavations, especially emergency ones where sites in the area suddenly become available between demolition and redevelopment. There is a Fieldwork Group which meets regularly to discuss policy and organize recording visits. The Society's work covers the history of Southwark and Lambeth from prehistoric to industrial times.

To join, write to the Secretary, whose name you can get from the Cuming Museum. Membership is open to anyone keen to take an active part, and there are meetings on most nights of the week for practical work, such as pot washing, classifying and labelling.

THE MONUMENTAL BRASS SOCIETY, c/o The Society of Antiquaries of London, Burlington House, Piccadilly, W1.

London is particularly good for brass rubbing. One way of getting experience is to rub pavement man-hole covers – most districts have decorative Victorian covers to choose from. Remember that permission from the vicar is needed before you do any brass rubbing in a church. You will probably be expected to pay a small fee or contribute to church funds.

The above Society, which you may want to get in touch with if you become really interested in brasses, has no permanent address, but if you write to the Honorary Secretary, c/o The Society of Antiquaries, your letter will be forwarded.

Materials and equipment for brass rubbing can be bought at Phillips and Page, 50 Kensington Church Street, W8. They also sell a useful pamphlet, *Where to Go Brass Rubbing in the Greater London Area*. The equipment needed to get started is simple and inexpensive.

Scientific

THE BRITISH ASSOCIATION FOR THE ADVANCEMENT OF SCIENCE, Sanctuary Buildings, 20 Great Smith Street, SW1 [799 – 7657].

Founded in 1831, this Association is today the only national scientific body concerned with all scientific and technological disciplines, and with the presentation of science and technology (including their impact upon society) to scientists, technologists and non-scientists alike, of all ages and in all walks of life. A special organization, British Association Young Scientists (12 to 18 years), caters for young people, and there are a number of branches in the London area. For further particulars about the Association and how to become involved in its activities, write to the secretary at the above address.

BLACKHEATH SCIENTIFIC SOCIETY, Honorary Secretary, Mr Nurse, 43a Burnt Ash Road, SE12 [852 – 2308]. Annual membership 75p.

The Society meets once a month between October and May at the Kidbrooke Community Centre, Greenwich. Meetings are addressed by guest speakers who cover a variety of scientific topics; talks are normally illustrated by slides or films. At two recent meetings talks on hydrofoils and crime detection were given. To join write to the Honorary Secretary, and your application will be considered by the committee.

HAMPSTEAD SCIENTIFIC SOCIETY, Honorary Secretary, H. Stark, 5a Belsize Park Gardens, NW3 [722 – 5918]. Annual membership £1.

The Hampstead Scientific Society was founded in 1899. One of its chief attractions is the Society's Observatory, which contains a six-inch refractory telescope, the only one available in London to the general public. It is sited at Lower Terrace, and can be used every clear Saturday evening between 8 and 10 p.m. from 1 October to the end of April. There is always a member demonstrator on duty.

The Society, which aims to promote local interest in all branches of science, meets at 8 p.m. on one Thursday a month at the Medical Research Laboratory, on Holly Hill. A talk given by a guest speaker who is a specialist in a particular scientific subject is followed by coffee and a general discussion. The Society's activities include a yearly scientific film-show by Mullard Ltd, excursions to places of scientific interest, geological expeditions and expeditions to the Heath to study its animal, bird and plant life.

THE ROYAL INSTITUTION OF GREAT BRITAIN, 21 Albemarle Street, W1 [493 – 0669 and 5716].

Membership of the Royal Institution is open to anyone who is interested in science. No special scientific qualification is required, but applications for membership must normally be sponsored by four members. The entrance fee is £3·15, and the annual subscription £7·35. There is a special membership category, Associate Subscriber, for young people (17–27), who are welcomed by the Institution. The annual subscription for Associates under 23 is £2·10, over 23 £4·20.

The Royal Institution, founded in 1799, has a long and distinguished history in the world of scientific research. 21

Albemarle Street, its original home, remains a meeting place for scientists as well as an active centre for scientific research. The functions of the Royal Institution are twofold; to extend scientific knowledge by means of research in the Davy-Faraday Research Laboratory, and to facilitate a wider understanding of science and its methods through lecturing and publishing activities. Members can use the library and reading room, and attend the Friday evening discourses, discussions and other lectures. For many years a special feature of the Institution's activities (and one for which it is famous) has been the Christmas lectures for young people; a course of six lectures on a particular subject given during the Christmas holidays each year. It is not necessary to be a member to attend these lectures. For details of tickets write to the Secretary at 21 Albemarle Street.

LONDON NATURAL HISTORY SOCIETY. Annual subscription £2·50.

The Society has a full programme of meetings, excursions and rambles, which cover all aspects of natural history under the general headings of ornithology, ecology, entomology, botany, geology and archaeology. To apply for membership write to the Membership Secretary, Mr A. J. Barrett, 40 Frinton Road, Kirby Cross, Frinton on Sea, Essex.

The Society has a library at the Central Library (Reference Department), Walpole Park, Ealing, W 5. Members can use the library on tickets issued by the Membership Secretary. Two journals, the *London Naturalist* and *London Bird Report*, are sent annually to all members.

THE ZOOLOGICAL SOCIETY OF LONDON, Regent's Park, NW1 [722 – 3333].

The Society is a scientific society. If you are interested in becoming a member further details can be obtained from the Membership Registrar. There are three classes of elected membership: Scientific Fellows who must be zoologists and recommended for election by three Fellows of the Society; Ordinary Fellows who must be sponsored, also by three Fellows of the Society; and Associates, who apply for election but do not need sponsors. The annual subscription for Associates is £5, and membership entitles you to attend scientific meetings and symposia, to visit the

London Zoo and Whipsnade free, to use the members' restaurant, and to apply for a ticket to use the library.

THE SOCIETY FOR PSYCHICAL RESEARCH, 1 Adam and Eve Mews, W8 [937 – 8984]. Annual subscription £3·15.

The Society holds regular meetings for the reading and discussion of papers on all aspects of psychical research. There is a library of books, pamphlets and periodicals relating not only to psychical research but also to such subjects as philosophy, psychology and hypnotism. The library is open from Monday to Friday, 10 a.m.–5 p.m., but is closed during August.

THE ROYAL GEOGRAPHICAL SOCIETY, Kensington Gore, SW7 [589 – 0648].

The Society helps to further geographical work, especially through its support of expeditions, and is a centre for geographical research and information. Fellowship is worthwhile if you are really interested, and entitles you to attend meetings and use the extensive library and Map Room, for which you must be 21. Application for Fellowship must be sponsored by a Fellow through personal knowledge or, if you are a student applying for Associate Membership, by your school, university or parents. Entrance fee £4·20, annual subscription £6·30. Associate membership is open to those between 16 and 21 at an annual subscription of £2. For further details write to The Director and Secretary at the above address.

BRITISH ASTRONOMICAL ASSOCIATION, Burlington House, Piccadilly, W1 [734 – 4145]. Annual subscription £3·25, under 21 £2·50.

Membership of the Association is open to anyone interested in astronomy. You write to the secretary and ask for a form. Your application must be sponsored by either one member, or two householders, known to you personally.

The Association encourages amateur astronomical observation, publishes worthwhile findings and does all it can to stimulate public interest in astronomy. Members meet on the last Wednesday of every month from October to June at 23 Saville Row, W1. Members' papers are read, talks are given and tea is provided. The Association publishes a *Journal* and a *Handbook*, the cost of which is covered by the annual subscription.

There is a library at Burlington House, and also a collection of lantern slides, film-strips and photographs. Members can use the library on Wednesdays and borrow, by arrangement, books, instruments and photographic material. Members work together in sections to carry out practical observation projects.

THE BRITISH INTER-PLANETARY SOCIETY, 12 Bessborough Gardens, SW1 [828– 9371]. Annual membership £4·50 (16 years and over), students £3·50.

The Society was founded in 1933 to encourage advances in space science and technology. Although membership will obviously be more rewarding for those really interested in the subject, many non-technical meetings are held in London during the year which are open to the public. These often include film shows. Other main meetings last for several days and deal with special aspects of the subject. Outstanding events usually take the form of a special Presentation Meeting, often addressed by astronauts or other space personalities.

Your subscription entitles you to attend all meetings and to receive, monthly, either the Society's *Journal,* or their magazine, *Spaceflight.*

6

A SECOND CHANCE

Many people, for a variety of reasons, want to carry on or go back to their studies after they have left school. If you are one of them, it is comforting to know that London offers splendid chances for part-time further education.

You can work for O level and A level examinations, for degrees and for the qualifications required by various professional bodies. Or, of course, you can study without any particular qualification in mind, just because you enjoy it. Certainly, it is easier and more practical to get the qualifications you want while you are still in full-time education. For one thing, you don't have to do another job all day. For another you may find, once you have started, that you really need a grant to carry on – it's harder to get one after you have left school and taken a job than while you are still at school or college. Nevertheless thousands of people *do* qualify successfully at various levels as a result of part-time study. Determination to succeed in your chosen subject will make up for the lack of time available, and any other difficulties.

The aim of this chapter is to outline the facilities in London, and to suggest where you can find help and advice.

GUIDANCE

Before starting on an examination course you may like to take advice from a specialist centre for vocational guidance. Alternatively, if you think that your evening classes may eventually lead to your wanting to attend a university or polytechnic full-time to work for a degree, you will need the best advice available in selecting which A levels to take, and ultimately in deciding which university to apply to. Your teacher or lecturer will probably be able to give all the advice you need but if you want special detailed information there are firms that offer reliable Educational and Career advice.

The following bodies give information on a number of different levels.

THE YOUTH EMPLOYMENT SERVICE is a free service run in London by the Inner London Education Authority, and in the Outer London boroughs by the local education authorities. There are Youth Employment Offices in all districts, and they will help anyone under 18, or older if still at school, to choose and find a job or get information about training for work after leaving full-time school. The address of your local Youth Employment Office can be found in the telephone directory, or at the nearest Employment Exchange or post office.

OCCUPATIONAL GUIDANCE UNITS are designed to help anyone of any age whether in full-time education (except school) or not. Their particular task is to advise people who for one reason or another feel unsettled in their present employment and want information about other suitable jobs, or want to find out how they can get further training, especially while working at a full-time job. If you think that an interview would be useful, phone your nearest Occupational Guidance Unit – you can get the number at the local Employment Exchange.

HER MAJESTY'S STATIONERY OFFICE publishes a series of career booklets which give basic information about the entry qualifications required, the length of the training period, and the opportunities offered by a variety of careers. The booklets can be obtained from any branch of the Stationery Office. They are sometimes brought up to date and reprinted, so it is important to make sure you get the latest edition.

GABBITAS-THRING EDUCATIONAL TRUST LTD, Advisory Service, 6 Sackville Street, W1 [734 – 0161].

Advice is given about private tuition for O levels and A levels, and details about language and other courses at private schools and colleges in the London area are provided. Most of these courses are designed for foreign students learning English, but there are also foreign language classes at various levels for English students.

TRUMAN & KNIGHTLEY EDUCATIONAL TRUST, 91–3 Baker Street, W1 [486 – 0931].

The Trust gives advice about language and other schools, and also runs an advisory service on certain aspects of further education, in particular O and A levels. As part of this service some educational guides are available.

Titles include: *Full-Time Degree Courses at Colleges of Higher Education* (27½p post free); *Grants for Higher Education* (52½p postage 5p); *Which University?* (published annually by Cornmarket Press, £2·50 post free).

The following two organizations are not cheap but they will make a very detailed examination of your interests and abilities and if you really are at a loss as to what to do they can come up with some interesting ideas.

THE TAVISTOCK INSTITUTE OF HUMAN RELATIONS, Tavistock Centre, 120 Belsize Lane, NW3 [435 – 7111].

Guidance takes the form of a series of interviews designed to help the individual appraise his own abilities. The results of aptitude and intelligence tests play an important part in the discussions with interviewers. Cost: around £25.

NATIONAL INSTITUTE OF INDUSTRIAL PSYCHOLOGY, 14 Welbeck Street, W1 [935 – 1144].

The normal session of one and a half days is particularly meant to help young people and students. The whole day is set aside for aptitude and intelligence tests, the half day for interviews. The Institute deals with people interested in careers in the professions, trades or business. The standard procedure can be amended for older people according to individual circumstances. Cost: £25.

NATIONAL ADVISORY CENTRE ON CAREERS FOR WOMEN, 251 Brompton Road, SW3 [589 – 9237].

NACCW is an educational charity which acts in an advisory capacity. The headquarters staff know a great deal about work open to women and the best way to set about training or applying for such work. They have done a lot to increase the opportunities for women, and are prepared to consider applications for modest interest-free loans for women who need some financial help in order to undertake a course of training that will fit them for useful and progressive work. Loans would cover such items as daily travel or the purchase of essential books.

For details of how to make use of the advice and services they offer get in touch with the Organizing Secretary at the above address. If you do decide to contact NACCW, you must be prepared to pay a fee of £3·15 for an interview, 50p for postal advice.

CAREERS FOR GIRLS. This is a useful book by Ruth Miller (revised edition Penguin 1970).

ADVISORY CENTRE FOR EDUCATION LTD, 32 Trumpington Street, Cambridge CB2 1QY [Cambridge 51456].

ACE publishes comprehensive booklets on particular subjects such as the content and emphasis of courses at different universities, the importance put on where you put a university in order of preference on your UCCA form, whether or not you can change your course at the end of your first year, and so on. The booklets cost £1·50 each, and should be in local libraries.

THE CAREERS RESEARCH AND ADVISORY CENTRE, Bateman Street, Cambridge [Cambridge 54445]. CRAC provides a careers advisory service through a series of publications and by a personal Question Service, which is operated on a fee-paying basis. The publications emphasize the bearing the choice of subjects at school, college and university has in an occupational context.

CRAC also publishes a series of booklets which compare in detail the first-degree courses available in various subjects at universities and colleges, and which help a prospective student to decide which course at which university sounds most appropriate.

EDUCATIONAL REDEPLOYMENT SERVICE, 20 Gower Street, London WC1 [637 – 0450].

Not everyone who starts on further or higher education after leaving school is lucky enough to find that they have chosen the right career. Every year thousands of students leave universities and colleges without having finished their courses.

The Educational Redeployment Service is an independent organization which was founded in 1969 with the object of helping students in all types of higher education who fail to complete their course of study. It is particularly concerned with students whose homes are in the London area. Its aim is to help such students to move into other educational channels more suited to their tastes and aptitudes, by providing information and advice about alternatives, particularly colleges of education and polytechnics. Any student who has given up a full-time degree course can make use of the Service by writing to it for information.

GRANTS

Grants are not normally given in connection with O and A levels, but beyond this stage help is usually offered towards the cost of full-time courses of study, provided that the applicant has resided in the United Kingdom for not less than three years immediately prior to the commencement of the course. As far as the authorities who provide the money are concerned, educational grants fall into two categories, mandatory and discretionary.

Local education authorities are obliged to offer financial help to those who have succeeded in getting a place at a university, college of education or establishment of similar status, to study for a first degree or qualification of comparable standard. If you obtain a place for an approved course of study – the approved courses are listed by the Department of Education and Science – your local education authority must make a grant towards your expenses. To apply you write direct to the education office of the borough in which you live (unless you live in Inner London in which case you should write to the ILEA, County Hall, SE1) giving details of your course, and where you are going to study.

In addition to the courses which appear on the Department's list there are other full-time recognized courses of higher education leading to specific professional qualifications which local education authorities recognize at their discretion. If you think that the course of study you propose to take falls into this category then you should get in touch with your local education officer and ask if you qualify for help. It must be stressed that in these cases grants are awarded at the discretion of the authority, and that they are normally available only to those undertaking full-time courses. It would be exceptional to be given help for a part-time course.

One very special branch of help deserves a mention here. About twenty-five mature state scholarships are awarded each year to students who must be over the age of twenty-five and who have failed to get a place in a university at the normal age, but who have subsequently shown that a university course would be valuable to them. Candidates for these awards are normally referred by an organization such as the Workers' Educational Association after having attended courses regularly for some time and if they have shown exceptional interest and ability.

The National Union of Students, 3 Endsleigh Street, WC1 [387 – 7227] publishes a booklet, *Educational Charities* (10p), which lists possible sources of help. Most of these charities have very limited funds, and can only offer loans, or small grants to help with expenses such as the cost of books.

THE INNER LONDON EDUCATION AUTHORITY

The ILEA runs part-time courses in 104 education centres of various kinds, and publishes a booklet every August called *Floodlight* (5p from GLC Information Centre, County Hall, SE1, or most bookstalls and newsagents), which gives a complete list of evening classes for the forthcoming year. Your public library will also have a list of facilities and classes offered by the institute in your district. Write to the Principal of your institute or college for a prospectus. He will also advise you, if necessary, about the kind of class suitable for your particular need. County Hall has an Education Inquiry Office which is open from Monday to Friday, 8.45 a.m.–5.15 p.m. If you want to telephone them ring County Hall [633 – 5000] and ask to be put through to the Education General Inquiry Office.

The ILEA's area covers the twelve boroughs of Inner London: Camden, Greenwich, Hackney, Hammersmith, Islington, Kensington and Chelsea, Lambeth, Lewisham, Southwark, Tower Hamlets, Wandsworth and Westminster. If you work in London but live outside these boroughs you can attend ILEA classes, but you may find that you have to pay a slightly higher fee than residents.

Details of classes available in Outer London can be obtained from the education officers of the Outer London boroughs. Each of the twenty boroughs is responsible for its own further education programme.

Classes at all ILEA education centres follow the academic year, September to July, and enrolment normally takes place during the third week in September. Fees vary according to the kind of class you attend. At most technical and commercial colleges, and colleges of further education, fees for a full session of three terms range between a £3 minimum for one or two evenings a week to a maximum fee of £6·75. At adult education and literary institutes the minimum fee is £2·75 for one class a week, rising to a maximum of £3·75 a week for four or more classes.

Educational qualifications

Public examination courses are offered at polytechnics, technical colleges, commercial colleges and colleges administered either by the local education authority or, in the case of Birkbeck College, by the University of London (see p. 131). For example, there are twenty-three centres at which O and A level courses in chemistry are offered, five where you can take a B.Sc. degree course, and six where you can study for higher degrees. If economics is your interest you can study up to A-level standard at twenty-six centres, and for a degree at five. In English you could do O and A level courses at forty-five centres, and study for a degree at two.

As part of the teaching of English offered in London, there are at least twenty-six centres where courses in Lower Cambridge and Cambridge Proficiency examinations for students from abroad are held. In certain districts specialist classes are organized to help groups of people with special language problems. Details of classes in English and foreign languages can be obtained from individual adult education institutes.

Professional training

Courses giving professional training in branches of business and technical work are the special concern of the polytechnics, technical and general and commercial colleges. For example, courses are given in such things as baking technology, hardware retailing, the inspection of meat and other foods, cabinet making, bookkeeping, bookbinding and photography. If you are going into the record industry and feel you should know as much as possible about your job, there are courses in high-fidelity sound reproduction and high-fidelity and tape recording.

Many of these courses prepare you for the City and Guilds examinations. When registering for a particular course, you should ask what qualification it could lead to.

Hobbies, interests and general manual skills

These are provided mainly by the adult education institutes and the literary institutes. The courses are not normally linked with specific examinations, but their scope is vast. You can attend classes on anything from Mandarin Chinese to scooter maintenance. They cater for such hobbies as sailing, eiderdown making, rug weaving, flower arrangement, filming or bird-watching. There are courses in art appreciation, as well as classes in all kinds of painting and drawing, music appreciation and music making, writing, journalism and many foreign languages at all levels. There are also classes in all branches of domestic science, car maintenance, painting and decorating, or indoor and outdoor gardening.

All these courses and many others are listed, with their place of study, in *Floodlight*.

ILEA day classes

Most of the adult education institutes administered by the ILEA hold a few day-time classes, geared, in the main, to meet the needs of married women and retired people. There are classes, for example, in dressmaking and keeping fit; also painting and creative studies, life modelling and carving, pottery, jewellery, screen painting, playgroup-leaders' course, motor cars (theory and practical), language classes in German, Italian and French. Most of the classes last either two or three hours.

If you have free time during the day it is worth calling at your local library or town hall to ask for the address of the nearest adult education institute, so that you can go along and find out what it has to offer during the day.

Some institutes hold day-time classes in general studies which carry with them no qualification, but which act as refresher courses for those who want to test their ability after a period away from academic work. The City Literary Institute, for example, has such a course, called 'Fresh Horizons', which could be of particular interest to anyone preparing to take a degree course with the Open University. (See p. 134.)

Day release classes

Some of the larger firms, and those of a rather specialized nature (e.g. printing, electricity, garages, civil service, optics, etc.) allow their employees to spend one day a week at a technical college or college for further education. Usually you have to work for an exam in the particular skill or trade in which you are employed, but some firms (e.g. the civil service) will allow you to prepare for GCE O or A level exams, and others may let you study with no exam in mind, just for 'general education' purposes. There is some evidence that not enough firms are aware of day release for 'general education' purposes, so you might need to give yours a gentle prod.

OTHER ORGANIZATIONS

UNIVERSITY OF LONDON DEPARTMENT OF EXTRA-MURAL STUDIES, 7 Ridgmount Street, WC1 [636 – 8000].

This Department provides further education in three main ways: University Extension Courses, University Tutorial Classes, and Summer and Weekend Schools. Classes are held at various

centres throughout London and are often arranged in co-operation with the local education authority or the Workers' Educational Association (see p. 133). Most of the classes take place
in the evenings, but some are held during the day. Most enrolment fees vary between £1·25 and £2 for the full session of two
terms, but there are a few courses for which the charge is
higher.

The Department of Extra-Mural Studies publishes a free
annual booklet, *University Classes for Adults*, which gives
information on all its courses for the coming academic year and
details of enrolment. Normally the only condition is that a
student should be eighteen years old or more, and generally
willing to attend regularly, take part in discussions in class, and
do the private reading and written work set by the tutor.

University Extension Courses are of two kinds – those leading
to a diploma or certificate, and those which do not entail any
examination, but involve studying at University level. Study for a
diploma involves attendance at four courses normally spread over
the same number of years, and that leading to a certificate
involves three years' attendance. Each course, lasting one year,
consists of twenty-four meetings. Diplomas are given in archaeology, biblical and religious studies, economics, film study, history,
history of art, history of music, international affairs, English
literature, sociology, visual arts, and science and transport
studies. There are also three-year Certificate Courses in crimino-
logy, film study and transport studies.

The diplomas are offered by the University as an indication that
a student has attended the classes regularly, and reached the
required standard in the examinations which are held at the end
of each year's work.

If you can satisfy the university entrance requirements – that
means, in fact, that you have at least three A levels and two O
levels – you can apply to study for the External Diploma in Social
Studies. This includes six months' practical work and is regarded
as a basic qualification. The academic part of the course can be
studied part-time.

University Tutorial Classes are of two types, one consisting of
twenty-four meetings, the other extending over three consecutive

years, each one of twenty-four meetings. All meetings last two hours, the groups are small, rarely exceeding twenty-four students, the seminar method is used and at least half of each meeting is devoted to discussion. There are no examinations, and no diplomas are offered, but students are given an opportunity to read widely round their subject, and written work is considered an important part of the course. The Tutorial Classes are nearly always arranged in cooperation with institutes of the ILEA or with the local WEA branch. Ask for details of courses in your district from the Secretary of the local WEA branch, the Principal of your local institute, or from the public library.

Tutorial Classes cater for a wide range of interests, for example: literature, history, sociology, philosophy, archaeology, science, economics, art appreciation and music appreciation. If sufficient interest is shown in a subject or an aspect of a subject, not covered by any class, the Department will try to meet the demand.

A few *Summer and Weekend Schools* are arranged each year. Write to 7 Ridgmount Street, WC1 for details of the subjects to be covered, dates and places of each course.

In addition many residential courses are organized throughout the year at centres all over the country. The courses are sponsored by a variety of organizations, and cover a wide range of interests. The National Institute of Adult Education, 35 Queen Anne Street, London W1M 0BL [580 – 3155] publishes, twice yearly, a calendar called *Residential Short Courses*, which lists the courses in date order giving a short, one-line description of the topic, the place, the name of the sponsoring body from whom details can be had, and the cost. Write to NIAE headquarters at the above address, enclosing 15p, if you want a copy of the calendar.

WORKERS' EDUCATIONAL ASSOCIATION, London District Office, 32 Tavistock Square, WC1 [387 – 8966].

The WEA has nearly eighty branches in the London district. Their activities include courses of classes, weekend and summer schools, educational visits, rambles, lectures, theatre visits and socials. Most of the classes are organized in co-operation with the London University Department of Extra-Mural Studies (see p. 131) or with the local education authority.

Classes normally start at 7 p.m. and last until 9 p.m. Cooperation between tutor and students is encouraged; thus, as in many adult education classes, the syllabus for any one course is not necessarily fixed until suggestions from students have been considered.

If you want to know more about the WEA write to the above address, or to the Membership Secretary, Central London Branch, 19 Howard Court, Peckham Rye, SE15. The branch membership fee is 50p a year, but if you join a class, the course fee includes the membership fee. Membership entitles you to receive the Branch Bulletin, the Class Programme and the Annual Report.

THE OPEN UNIVERSITY, London Regional Office, 21 Gloucester Place, W1 [486 – 6733].

The Open University is concerned, except in special circumstances, only with students over the age of 21 who are in fulltime employment or working in the home. No formal academic qualification of any kind is demanded as a condition of acceptance for any of its courses. However, if you have not been attending adult education classes with any organization, the ILEA, the WEA or the University of London Department of Extra-Mural Studies, for example, you may feel doubtful about your ability to embark on a course of study that will eventually reach degree level. For people who think they may need to undertake some form of preparatory course the BBC, in collaboration with the National Extension College, Cambridge (see p. 136), offers courses in three fields, mathematics, literature, and history and social psychology. Write to The National Extension College, Room U, 8 Shaftesbury Road, Cambridge for details of these courses, which are called *Square Two*, *Reading to Learn* and *Man in Society*.

Applications for admission should be addressed to: Admissions, The Open University, P.O. Box 48, Walton, Bletchley, Bucks. Although the University insists, on principle, that anyone may register for its courses of study, regardless of academic qualification, it must, and does, use a process of selection in the case of courses which are over-subscribed. It is possible, therefore, that your application to register may not at first be accepted.

Fees. A provisional registration fee of £10 is payable when your application to register for one or more courses is accepted. It covers the cost of registration and about three months of your first correspondence course.

The remaining fee for each foundation course is £10, plus a fee of £25 or £30 to cover the expenses of attendance at summer school or weekend courses. The fee for courses at second, third and fourth levels is £20 per course. The University estimates that the cost of a B.A. degree will be in the region of £140, a B.A. degree with honours, £180. Fees will, of course, be spread over a period of three or four years.

Courses of Study. The Open University awards its own degree, as described above. To obtain a B.A. degree you must get credits in six of the courses offered by the University, two of which must be foundation courses. For an honours degree you will require eight credits, two in foundation courses. Courses are organized at four levels of academic study, and students must obtain a credit in at least one course at each level before applying for a course at a more advanced level. It is not necessary to undertake to study for a degree when you apply for admission. However, if you wish to study only one or two of the courses, then you should make it clear on your application form that you are not seeking a degree.

The Open University has courses in six faculties: arts, mathematics, science, social studies, educational studies and technology. Tuition is organized on the basis of correspondence courses, and each course consists of correspondence 'packages' containing assignments to be completed and returned by the student. Series of radio and television programmes supplement the correspondence courses, and the foundation courses include attendance at a summer school lasting for up to two weeks, which is regarded as an integral part of the course, and which is compulsory except in very special circumstances.

Study centres, where face-to-face tuition in groups takes place every few weeks, are also considered an essential part of the courses. A personal counsellor is in attendance most evenings and you can ask his advice on matters arising from your study. There are about ten study centres in Inner London, and another twenty-seven in the rest of the London region. For details of the

London study centres write to the Regional Director at the above address.

The Open University publishes a prospectus which gives addresses of regional headquarters, full details of courses and plans for the future. Write to the headquarters at Bletchley if you want a copy.

ILEA grants. Students living in Inner London are elegible for a minimum grant of £25 from the ILEA towards Open University fees for one foundation course, and £30 if they are taking two courses. The grants cover the cost of the summer schools students have to attend, but cannot be used for the registration fee of £10. The ILEA regards the payment of the fee by the student himself as being an indication of serious intent. If you live in one of the Outer London boroughs and want to apply for a grant in connection with Open University studies, you should apply direct to the local education officer in your area.

THE NATIONAL EXTENSION COLLEGE, 8 Shaftesbury Road, Cambridge, CB2 2BP [0223 – 63465].

The National Extension College provides correspondence courses at O and A level in a variety of subjects, and degree and diploma courses. The bulk of the work is done by correspondence, but many of the courses are linked with radio and television programmes. The NEC works in close cooperation with the Open University (see p. 134), especially in preparing students who have not studied for many years to come to terms with the amount of work involved in getting a degree without attending a formal university.

Quite apart from the correspondence courses aimed at the achievement of an academic, professional or technical qualification, the NEC has one or two courses of general interest, for example 'Child Development – You and Your Child', and another called 'Playgroups', a course designed to help a parent who wants to start a playgroup in her area.

Details of all the courses offered by the NEC, together with fees, can be had from their office in Cambridge.

PRIVATE SCHOOLS AND COLLEGES.

There are a large number of private schools offering courses of study in various subjects. They advertise widely in underground stations and the press, and their telephone numbers and addresses can be found easily in the telephone directory (yellow pages). The most numerous are the secretarial schools, where you can get tuition in shorthand, typing and other business skills. Language schools also abound. These cater mainly for foreign students who want to learn English, but many of them do run courses in such languages as French, German, Spanish and Italian. At some colleges you can also take O and A level courses in various academic subjects.

Private colleges usually manage to teach students in small groups, and at their best they can be very good. But they are expensive, and it may take you longer to achieve the standard you are after than you bargained for. It is wise, before you start, to try to find out just how much your course is likely to cost you, and also to compare what is offered by different schools.

THE METHODIST YOUTH DEPARTMENT.

This has a training centre at 5 Crestfield Street, WC2 [278 – 2013], where it combines 'catch-up' academic courses for early school leavers with youth leadership training. The academic part of the training is carried out in cooperation with the Kingsway College of Further Education. It is not necessary to be a member of the Methodist church to apply for admission to one of these courses.

THE YOUNG WOMEN'S CHRISTIAN ASSOCIATION OF GREAT BRITAIN, 2 Weymouth Street, W1 [636 – 9722/6].

The YWCA organizes residential courses several times a year lasting five days, and normally held at Walsingham House, Forest View, Chingford. The courses, called Blue Triangle Residential Courses for Young Workers, are for girls between the ages of 15 and 20 who are in their first year or so at work. The aim of the courses is to stimulate interest in art, politics, theatre, current affairs and so on. There are lectures, discussion groups, visits to central London and places of interest such as the Port of London, the Television Centre and newspaper offices. The five-day course is recognized by the Duke of Edinburgh Award Office.

Individual applications for the courses are not accepted. Girls who attend are nominated and sponsored by their firms, so if you think such a course would help and interest you, you will have to ask your employer to put your name forward.

THE ELECTRICAL ASSOCIATION FOR WOMEN, 25 Foubert's Place, W1 [437 – 5212]. Annual subscription 37½p.

The main purpose of the EAW is electrical education. Members, through meetings, publications, discussion groups and visits are kept informed of the latest developments in electrical apparatus for domestic use. There are over 260 branches, and each branch organizes its own activities. At its headquarters in London the EAW runs two courses of special practical interest. One, a three-session course, is for women. You learn how to read a meter, how to mend a fuse and how to wire a plug. The other course is a cookery one – and it is for men only.

The Association also administers the Caroline Haslett Memorial Trust, which enables it to award bursaries, scholarships and exhibitions to women who wish to make a career in the electrical industry.

THE WINSTON CHURCHILL MEMORIAL TRUST, 10 Queen Street, W1.

This Trust was founded to enable men and women, who might otherwise not have the chance, to travel abroad, and widen their knowledge in their own field of activity.

Help is given in the form of travelling Fellowships designed to meet the cost of travel, living expenses, fees and other expenses during a period of between three and twelve months. The average grant amounts to about £1,500. No age limit is set, and no special qualifications are required. The Fellowships are awarded to people engaged in almost any kind of work or activity. In 1970, for example, the categories from which Fellows were chosen included adventure, sport, care of the aged, school teaching, glass and ceramic design and manufacture as well as many others.

For details of the scheme, including information about how to apply for a Fellowship, write to the Trust at the above address.

7

HELP, I NEED SOMEBODY

Doctor

Over the age of sixteen, you can choose your own doctor. There is a list of General Practitioners in most main post offices and public libraries or you can phone the Inner London Executive Council [837 – 7833] during office hours to find out names and addresses of local doctors. If you need treatment and haven't a doctor you can ask any General Practitioner to take you on his list as a temporary National Health Service patient.

In an emergency like flu, where a home visit is required and you haven't a GP, dial 100 for the operator or contact the nearest police station who will tell you the number of the nearest available doctor on call. You can also obtain treatment and medication by going to the nearest hospital with a casualty department.

Dentist

The Inner London Executive Council can also provide a list of dentists who are available under the National Health Service. If you're stricken with toothache at midnight or over the weekend when it's difficult to contact a dentist at his surgery, go to the casualty department of any of the large teaching hospitals, (listed under 'Hospitals' in the phone book), who will have a resident dental houseman.

All-night Chemists

BOOTS, Piccadilly Circus, W1 [930 – 4761].
JOHN BELL & CROYDEN, 50 Wigmore Street, W1 [935 – 5555].
H. D. BLISS, 50 Willesden Lane, NW6 [624 – 8000].

All-night Post Office

King William IV Street, Trafalgar Square, WC2 [930 – 9580].

LIFELINES

The following organizations all operate a telephone advice or counselling service, available twenty-four hours a day, seven days a week for those in need.

BIT [229 – 8219].

BIT is a listening, crisis, information and referral service which tends to cater for those who feel alienated from the more established forms of society. They try to cope with any problems including legal, medical and psychological emergencies and, if they can't help, they will direct you to someone who will. It is a twenty-four hour service but from approximately 10 p.m. to 10 a.m. they deal with real crises only, such as emergency accommodation, depression and 'bum trips'.

OPENLINE [930 – 1732].

This is a twenty-four-hour telephone service run by St Martin-in-the-Fields offering help to people in time of personal crisis. During the day their Social Service Unit is open at 5, St Martins Place, WC2 [930 – 4137]. Appointments are advisable.

RELEASE [Twenty-four-hour emergency, 603 – 8654; weekdays, 10 a.m.–6 p.m., 229 – 7753, 727 – 7753].

Release, a social-welfare bureau for young people, originally began to help drug-users but has now widened its scope to deal with other personal, social and legal problems.

SALVATION ARMY [236 – 5222].

The Salvation Army maintains a network of counsellors throughout London. This number is manned twenty-four hours a day at their headquarters and is available to people who find themselves in any sort of crisis situation. It is basically a telephone referral service.

THE SAMARITANS [626 – 9000].

The Samaritans help the suicidal and despairing. They offer the friendship of a fellow human being supplemented by counselling by a professional person or treatment by a doctor if necessary, but no caller is referred to another person without his consent. The contact is in complete confidence. Callers may remain anonymous and be befriended or counselled only over the telephone if they so wish. The majority accept an invitation to make personal contact.

The central London branch is at St Stephen's Church, Walbrook, EC5, behind the Mansion House. Other local branches are listed in the phone book.

THE STUDENT ADVISORY CENTRE [402 – 5233].

This service was started by the 18-year-old editor of *Student* magazine because the staff were getting so many requests from young people in need of help. Don't interpret 'student' too literally. In fact any young person can approach them. You may have seen their circular stickers 'Give Us Your Headaches' quoting an assortment from abortion, adoption, homosexuality, lesbianism, VD to psychiatric help, but they cope with lesser traumas too. They don't tackle these problems themselves but pass people on to more specialized professional sources of help.

YOUNG PEOPLE'S COUNSELLING SERVICES

Some local authorities are now running counselling services where young people, either living, studying or working in the borough, can call and discuss emotional problems with either a social worker or a doctor, someone specially interested in young people. You can always check if your borough has this sort of service by ringing the Social Services Department. The age range is usually between 16 and 25. The service is free.

BRENT CONSULTATION CENTRE, Johnston House, 51 Winchester Avenue, NW6 [328 – 0918].

There are sessions on Monday evenings from 7.30 p.m. to 10 p.m., on Thursday evenings from 7.30 p.m. to 10 p.m. and on Tuesday afternoons from 4.30 p.m. to 6 p.m. It saves waiting if you phone for an appointment.

YOUNG PEOPLE'S COUNSELLING SERVICE, Finsbury Health Centre, Pine Street, EC1 [837 – 0031] (Borough of Islington). Please phone for an appointment.

YOUTH COUNSELLING CENTRE, King's Road Clinic, Richmond [977 – 4411].

Sessions are held on Thursday evenings from 5.30 to 7.30 p.m. and it is preferable to make an appointment.

WESTMINSTER YOUTH ADVISORY CLINIC.

Phone the Health Department [828 – 8070] for an appointment. The Wednesday afternoon session (2–4.30 p.m.) is held at 31 Nottingham Place, W1 (off Marylebone Road, nearly opposite Madame Tussauds). The Tuesday evening session (5–7 p.m.) is at the Maternity and Child Welfare Clinic, Pickering House, Hallfield Estate, W2.

The following are counselling services available to all young people regardless of borough boundaries:

LONDON YOUTH ADVISORY CENTRE, 31 Nottingham Place, W1 [935 – 8870].

This Centre offers a counselling service to young people confronted with sexual and emotional problems including, where appropriate, birth control, medical or legal advice. There is a small fee. Phone for an appointment.

THE YOUNG PEOPLE'S COUNSELLING SERVICE, Tavistock Centre, Belsize Lane, NW3 [435 – 7111].

This Service provides free and confidential counselling help to young people. Experience shows that it is most suitable for those aged between 17 and 21, though people slightly older and younger are also seen. It is staffed by professional workers trained to help understand the problems of the young. The aim is to provide a setting in which young people can talk over and be helped to understand better their personal concerns. It is not a service appropriate for those requiring medical or psychiatric help. Appointments may be made by phone or letter.

Another department at the Tavistock Centre deals with Vocational Guidance (see p. 125).

THE BLENHEIM PROJECT, 269a Portobello Road, W11 [727 – 3163].

This is staffed by professional social workers and caters for young drifters coming to London from other parts of the country. The aims are primarily casework with those who are able to accept it. Others find the premises a comfortable warm place to sit where there is always free tea or coffee, and a bath with soap and clean towels provided. Emergency accommodation for two to three nights may be made available as well as the usual professional help – legal, medical and psychiatric. The Project offers an accepting atmosphere where young people can 'be' with the possibility of receiving help if they desire it. The age range is roughly 16–21.

OTHER COUNSELLING SERVICES WITH NO AGE LIMITS

THE FAMILY PLANNING ASSOCIATION, 27 Mortimer Street, W1 [636 – 9135].

At the Information Bureau, open between 11 a.m. and 3 p.m., callers may have a private consultation with a specially trained information secretary. Abortion, desertion, divorce, homosexuality and pregnancy are just some of the difficulties which they can advise you about.

WELFARE ADVISORY SERVICE FOR NURSES, 1a Henrietta Place, W1 [580 – 2646].

The Royal College of Nursing and the National Council of Nurses of the UK run an advisory service for nurses and student nurses, male and female. You don't have to be a member of the RCN to ask the Welfare Adviser for help. She can sometimes put people in financial difficulty in touch with an appropriate trust fund, and can advise unmarried nurses with babies, and nurses who have had breakdowns and may be reluctant about returning to work. She will also advise on other personal problems.

WESTMINSTER PASTORAL FOUNDATION, The Central Hall, Westminster, SW1 [930 – 6676/7]. (Entrance in Matthew Parker Street, or through lounge in the Westminster Rooms of the Central Hall.)

Open from Monday to Friday, 10 a.m.–6 p.m., providing a counselling service in personal, marital and family problems. Appointments should be made by phone or letter. Counselling sessions normally last forty-five to fifty minutes. People who come to the foundation for long-term therapy are expected to contribute according to their means, but help to an individual is never governed by financial considerations.

All the previously mentioned 'umbrella' advisory services will pass people on to specialized help if necessary. Anyone with a clearly defined problem can always go direct.

SPECIALIZED SOURCES OF HELP

Alcoholism

INFORMATION CENTRE, Church of St Mary Woolnoth [626 – 9701], on the corner of King William Street and Lombard Street, EC3. (Right over Bank underground station.)

This Centre gives advice and help to anyone living or working in the City; they may have a drinking problem themselves, or else be a relative or employer of someone who has. Open 10 a.m.–5 p.m.

OXENDEN PRESBYTERIAN CHURCH, Haverstock Hill, NW3.

A walk-in clinic is held here on Thursday evenings from 6 to 8 p.m. with a doctor in attendance. You don't need an appointment. Just go. (This is the new location of the New Gallery Clinic which used to be in Regent Street.)

See also Alcoholics Anonymous, p. 149.

Disablement

INFORMATION SERVICE FOR THE DISABLED, Disabled Living Foundation, 346 Kensington High Street, W14 [602 – 2491].

Specific inquiries, such as where wheelchairs can be hired or what specialized equipment is available to the disabled, are dealt with. They also have a permanent exhibition of aids which can be seen by appointment.

A useful book is Freda Bruce Lockhart's *London for the Disabled*, published by Ward Lock and Co. Ltd. (30p) which lists hotels, pubs, theatres and shops which have access for the disabled.

Marital problems

THE TAVISTOCK CENTRE, Belsize Lane, NW3 [435 – 7111].

The Centre has a Marital Unit for the psychotherapeutic treatment of difficulties in marriage. This is part of the National Health Service, and consultations have to be arranged initially through a doctor. There may be a wait for a vacancy. Both partners must be willing to come.

LONDON MARRIAGE GUIDANCE COUNCIL, 76a New Cavendish Street, W1 [580 – 1087].

They will make an appointment for you with one of their counsellors. These confidential interviews will not take place in your home but on neutral territory, and it isn't necessary for both partners to be seen. Even if a couple have already decided on separation or divorce, they will still be helped to adjust to the situation.

CATHOLIC MARRIAGE ADVISORY COUNCIL, 33 Willow Place, SW1 [828 – 8307].

Marriage counselling is available by appointment. People wanting information and advice about birth regulation, as well as people with sexual difficulties, can be given an appointment with a doctor.

JEWISH MARRIAGE EDUCATION COUNCIL, 529b Finchley Road, NW3 [794 – 5222].

They will arrange a day or evening appointment with a counsellor at a mutually convenient place in London. They make a point of seeing people within a day or so.

Migraine

THE CITY MIGRAINE CLINIC, 11–12 Bartholomew Close, EC2 [606 – 1643].

Open Mondays to Fridays, 10 a.m.–4 p.m. Patients attending must have a letter of referral from their family doctor unless they are having an acute attack in which case emergency treatment will be given by the doctor on duty. Rest facilities are available after treatment.

Sexual problems

THE ALBANY TRUST, 32 Shaftesbury Avenue, W1 [734 – 5588 and 734 – 0960].

Help is given to both men and women who have sexual problems, including homosexuals, whether those problems are legal, medical, psychological or social. Ring or write for an appointment with their social worker.

Stammerers

Details of speech therapy classes especially for people who stammer are given in *Floodlight*, the guide to evening classes published by the ILEA in the autumn. You may need psychotherapy to overcome an acute stammer and your GP can give you a note of referral to an out-patient unit.

Drugs

The prescribing of 'hard' drugs is officially restricted to registered doctors working in Drug Treatment Centres, attached to many of the large teaching hospitals. Here drug-users are kept on minimum maintenance dosage, and, if they wish, may be admitted for voluntary in-patient treatment to an Addiction Unit. Different Treatment Centres cope with different kinds of addiction; some see only heroin addicts. Any GP should be able to tell you the appropriate clinic to go to whether you are a patient of his or not.

As Drug Treatment Centres are only open during the day at certain hours, anyone in a crisis outside those hours should go to the nearest hospital casualty department.

Anyone becoming over-dependent on other drugs, such as amphetamines, barbiturates or cannabis should also seek medical help. GPs vary in their knowledge and interest in the subject but one of the counselling or advisory services mentioned earlier should be able to pass you on to the best source of help.

COMMUNITY DRUG PROJECT, Burnett Hall, Wren Road, SE5 [701 – 0294].

The project runs a day centre in Camberwell for young people with drug problems, which is open five days a week; Mondays, 10 a.m.–8 p.m., Tuesday to Friday, 10 a.m.–4 p.m. Its aim is to provide the first stage of a rehabilitation programme by helping people in their resolve to give up not only drugs but also the way of live involved.

THE NATIONAL ADDICTION AND RESEARCH INSTITUTE is a registered charity which in addition to research and preventive programmes runs a day centre, as a therapeutic community, where patients are weaned from drugs by being given oral substitutes and then treated by group therapy of various kinds. No fees are charged. No injectable substances are prescribed and preference is given to patients of younger age groups. There is usually a waiting list but inquiries can be made [352 – 1590].

Drug dependence is a medical matter but as the possession of any drugs, hard or soft, other than those obtained on prescription is illegal, then inevitably the law is involved as well.

RELEASE, 40 Princedale Road, W11 [Twenty-four-hour emergency, 603 – 8654; weekdays 10 a.m.–6 p.m. 229 – 7753, 727 – 7753]. Late nights, Monday and Thursday.

Release was established to help young people charged with drug offences. They provide advice on individual rights regarding search, arrest and court procedure. A twenty-four-hour telephone service operates enabling those in urgent need of advice or assistance to talk directly to volunteers. They issue a printed card giving instructions on what to do if arrested, useful to keep with you.

After-care facilities for ex-drug-users are hopelessly inadequate. Release can occasionally help with accommodation and also by way of personal contact. Because the people at Release are young the service is informal and approachable.

Some useful publications are *Pot or Not* and *Behind the Drug Scene*, both 12½p each including postage, from Family Doctor House, 47–51 Chalton Street, NW1; *Drugs* by Peter Laurie, a Penguin Special (22½p).

Supplementary benefit

You may at some time, through illness, losing a job or some other reason, find yourself in financial difficulties, and in need of

Supplementary Benefit. In order to apply, you can either go in person to the local area office (the nearest post office will tell you the address and office hours), or you can fill in and post form S1, obtainable from the post office. You will then be visited at home and your case discussed. People able to work, i.e., not sick and with no dependents preventing them from working should claim on form B1 which is held at Employment Exchanges. They too will be interviewed at home or in case of urgent need they can take the form themselves to the local social security office. Students on grants are not normally eligible for benefit, nor are people not resident in this country.

Payments are usually made by Giro which, if there are delays in the post, can cause difficulty. Immediate cash payments can however be made in cases of urgent need. All London area offices are closed on Saturdays but the London Emergency Office, 96 Great Guildford Street, Southwark, SE1 [928 – 6870] keeps the following hours: Mondays to Fridays, 4.30–10.45 p.m.; Saturdays 11.30 a.m.–10 p.m.; Sundays and Public Holidays, 10.30 a.m.–10 p.m.

The Supplementary Benefits Commission are rather like Income Tax collectors in that they don't go out of their way to help you claim the maximum allowance available to you. Much of their help is discretionary and subject to a secret unpublished 'A' code to which even social workers don't have access. If you feel you have been unfairly treated by the Supplementary Benefits Commission, you can always go to your local Citizens' Advice Bureau (see p. 163) who get a lot of queries on this subject. They can often sort out a misunderstanding with the local area office manager.

A Supplementary Benefits Handbook, published by HMSO (32½p) is really intended for social workers, but it does give a useful background to the workings of the Supplementary Benefits Commission and includes a chapter on the right to appeal and how to go about it. The Child Poverty Action Group, 1 Macklin Street, WC2 publishes *A Guide to Supplementary Benefit Appeal* (5p). *A Guide to Social Security* is a free booklet which should be available from social security offices.

Claimants' Union

All the members of a Claimants' Union know what it's like to be on the receiving end of social security because they are all claimants themselves or have recently been so. They will go along with a new claimant to help represent them at an Appeals Tribunal.

The Claimants' Union campaigns against various injustices: the refusal of the Supplementary Benefits Commission to pay a full rent allowance which, with London's high rents, causes particular hardship; the policy which tries to force unmarried mothers and deserted wives to sue for maintenance as a condition of receiving help; and the secrecy of the 'A' code, which results in a great disparity of help. There are three Claimants' Unions in London so far: West London Claimants' Union, 10 Silchester Road, W 11 [229 – 6729] 1–5 p.m.; East London Claimants' Union Centre, Dame Colet House, Ben Jonson Road, E 1 [790 – 3867]; North London Claimants' Union, 17 Duncombe Road, N19.

SELF-HELP GROUPS

Professional help is valuable when it comes to diagnosing a personal problem. But treatment isn't always easily on hand after the crisis period is over. The individual is still left to learn how to live with his or her problem. The way in which self-help groups have mushroomed over recent years proves the value of the mutual support and encouragement offered by fellow sufferers. The following are all self-help groups of people who have learned to help themselves and others at the same time.

ALCOHOLICS ANONYMOUS, 11 Redcliffe Gardens, S W 10.

The only requirement for A A membership is a desire by those who suffer from alcoholism to stop drinking. A A provides a means for the newcomer suffering from alcoholism to understand the nature of his problem, an opportunity to share the problem and his experience with fellow members, and offers a programme of recovery. Members may preserve their anonymity by using a Christian name only. There are no fees, and each group is self-supporting through its own contributions.

There are over sixty A A groups in the Greater London area.

To contact your nearest group phone London Enquiries Intergroup [352 – 1626]. After 10 p.m. they have an Answerphone service and if you leave your phone number or address, they will get in touch with you the next day.

AL-ANON FAMILY GROUPS, UK AND EIRE, c/o St Giles' Centre, Camberwell Church Street, SE5 [703 – 0397].

Al-Anon Family Groups are run quite separately from AA but aim to offer support to the families of alcoholics by group discussion in much the same way. In many cases the changed attitude of the family which comes from a better understanding of what alcoholism means, has resulted in the alcoholic eventually seeking the help of AA. For further information and address of nearest group, write to the General Secretary, or phone between 10 a.m. and 4 p.m., Mondays, Wednesdays or Fridays.

ALATEEN GROUPS sponsored by Al-Anon Family Groups are for young people aged 13–20 in whose homes there is a drinking problem. They meet at weekends. Phone 703 – 0397 as above for details of places and times.

GAMBLERS ANONYMOUS, c/o 19 Abbey House, Victoria Street, SW1 [222 – 4252, 24-hour answering service].

Some people find it difficult to accept compulsive gambling as an illness. Nevertheless it is, in spite of the fact that there are no obvious physical effects. Gamblers Anonymous work by group therapy in the same way as Alcoholics Anonymous. They adopt a similar 'just for today' message for their members, never making brave new promises for the future, but only for the next twenty-four hours. Their members come from all social classes and Christian names are used. Contact the above address for details of group meetings.

GAM-ANON, like Al-Anon, caters for the wives and relatives of compulsive gamblers. As with Al-Anon, it's often the fact of a wife joining first which leads a husband to seek help from Gamblers Anonymous. Write to or phone the same address as Gamblers Anonymous.

NATIONAL FEDERATION OF CLUBS FOR THE DIVORCED AND SEPARATED, c/o 126 Melrose Avenue, SW19.

Each club belonging to the National Federation is autonomous, electing its own committee and planning its own activities. These clubs provide a social outlet for people who may otherwise be reluctant to go out alone in the evenings, and yet desperately need the company of others. The atmosphere of a club where all the members share a common disrupting experience helps people to view their own situation with greater objectivity. Only separated and divorced people can be full members but any club can have an associate membership of up to 10 per cent of people who have been widowed. The Federation is always interested in hearing from people who would be willing to start a new club and can give advice about this. For further details write to the Club Membership Secretary, address as above.

NEUROTICS ANONYMOUS, 24 Carlton Hill, St Johns Wood, NW8 [624 – 6714].

This is the answer for those who have been told they ought to get out and meet more people, something which depressed or insecure people find difficult to do at the best of times. Members of Neurotics Anonymous are not officially sick, although many are recommended to come by their doctors. They are mostly intelligent lonely people suffering from the isolation of the individual in our present-day de-personalized environment. Many live alone in bedsitters.

NA meet three times a week: mid-week, Saturdays and Sundays. The first half of the meeting is usually a free, open and relaxed discussion on a topic of general interest, or else a talk by an invited speaker. After the refreshment break, there is an open forum on a wide variety of personal problems which members themselves suggest, and which are then discussed anonymously. First names only are used and both medical and lay people attend the meetings.

Membership of NA is £3·15 a year, plus a small contribution of 12½p whenever you go, which is towards the cost of hiring a room.

PHONOTACT, 37b Lilyville Road, SW6 [736 – 5594], is an organization concerned with counteracting the anonymity of life in a big city by giving people an opportunity to relate to others. They arrange for informal groups of around ten members to meet in each others' homes where activities can include anything from cookery to Yoga. Phonotact also puts people with similar interests in touch with each other and they introduce members living in the same locality.

You can ring their 24-hour Dial-a-Chat service on 828 – 5456. Membership is £5 a year. Every Monday, Tuesday and Wednesday there are free open meetings at 6.15 p.m. and 8.30 p.m. at the Grosvenor Hotel, Victoria, which provide a general background introduction to the scheme.

STOPPING SMOKING. Many local authority health departments run smoking clinic sessions from time to time. Ring up your local health department first to check. There is however a permanent clinic run by the Borough of Islington, at 32 Drayton Park, N5, off Holloway Road. Ring the Islington Health Department [359 – 0161] for further information. Anyone can go whether they live in the borough or not. The course lasts six weeks and is free. It is held on Tuesday evenings from 6 to 8 p.m.

WEIGHT WATCHERS, 2 Thames Street, Windsor, Berks [Windsor 69131].

Weight Watchers rely very much on the group therapy techniques used by the other self-help organizations. Their aim is to re-educate the eating habits of their members who must have a minimum of ten pounds to lose. Each member is supplied with a goal weight, appropriate to their age and height, together with a programme of eating. (They don't like the word 'diet' which implies going hungry.) No exercises or pills are involved.

They hold weekly group classes of mutual encouragement where slimmers compare experiences. Classes are usually mixed, but there is at least one separate male-only class. There is also a special children's and teenagers' class in North London. All the lecturers are successful weight losers. Registration costs £1·05 and each class costs 80p. You have to pay if you miss a class though you can drop out at any time.

Members who reach their goal weight are awarded a free life-membership. They must stay within two pounds of their goal weight and may attend one meeting a month without charge. Write to or phone the above address for a list of classes in your area. There are classes all over London and the UK.

SEX EDUCATION

The following organizations are all sources of information on sex and health education and preparation for marriage.

NATIONAL MARRIAGE GUIDANCE COUNCIL, 58 Queen Anne Street, W1 [935 – 2838].

A booklist of all their publications is available which also includes information on their marriage counselling services. The bookshop is open during the day. They also arrange discussion groups with young people in preparation for marriage. Write to the Education Secretary about this.

Similar work is done by the CATHOLIC MARRIAGE ADVISORY COUNCIL, Clitherow House, 15 Lansdowne Road, W11 [727 – 0141].

JEWISH MARRIAGE EDUCATION COUNCIL, 529b Finchley Road, NW3 [794 – 5222].

The Council holds regular group teach-ins as well as offering appointments for individual couples with a counsellor.

NATIONAL CHILDBIRTH TRUST, 9 Queensborough Terrace, W2 [229 – 9319].

The Trust runs classes for preparation for childbirth and seminars for ante-natal teachers. Study days for teachers engaged in Education for Parenthood include showings of available visual aids. Young People's Days are arranged in the Easter Holidays; usually parents apply on behalf of younger children but 16-year-olds and over can make their own application. There is a recommended book list and speakers are available for group meetings.

Family Doctor Booklets (12½p), published by the British Medical Association, are obtainable from Family Doctor House, 47–51 Chalton Street, NW1, and over the counter from some chemists. Send for their booklist to get an idea of the range, which covers various age groups.

Formal Aspects of Marriage (60p) is a *Which?* Supplement, explaining the procedure for a registry office or church wedding of any denomination. It also gives information on tax and insurance. Obtainable from the Consumers' Association, Caxton Hill, Hertford, or can be found in the reference section of most public libraries.

For people wanting to improve their sexual relationship with a partner there are two books written in dictionary form by a Danish couple, Inge and Sten Hegeler: *ABZ of Love* (52½p), published by Neville Spearman Ltd and *XYZ of Love* (£2), published by MacGibbon and Kee.

Contraception

No gypsy's warning but a gentle reminder that a babe-in-arms is likely to keep its mother fully occupied for the next sixteen years or so.

So Now You Know About Family Planning is a Family Doctor publication, which discusses and describes various methods.

Contraceptives is a *Which?* Supplement (£1) obtainable from the Consumers' Association, Caxton Hill, Hertford. You don't have to be a subscriber to *Which?* to buy this, and it is available in the reference sections of most public libraries.

BROOK ADVISORY CENTRES.

These centres were specially set up to offer contraceptive advice to the unmarrieds aged between 16 and 25. There are two full-time clinics in London, as well as sessions in various hospital out-patient departments, where young people can obtain contraceptives and discuss sexual or emotional difficulties with a doctor. An annual fee of £4 is charged which covers all visits for twelve months but there are special financial arrangements for people resident in certain boroughs whereby the borough pays the fee. Appointments are made through either of the full-time clinics: Tottenham Court Road Centre, 233 Tottenham Court Road, W1 [580 – 2991] and Walworth Centre, 55 Dawes Street, Off East Street, SE17 [703 – 9660].

FAMILY PLANNING ASSOCIATION, 27 Mortimer Street, W1 [636 – 9135].

All the clinics of the FPA offer advice to the unmarried as well as married people. The head office in Mortimer Street runs a Greater London Clinic Inquiry Service where you can phone for the address and times of your nearest clinic. There are around 200 in the London area. You ring the individual clinic to make an appointment. The annual fee for consultations is £3 which is sometimes met by the local authority of the borough in which you live. You do however have to pay for contraceptive supplies. Pregnancy testing is done at Mortimer Street and can be arranged through all branches. It costs £1·50.

MARIE STOPES MEMORIAL CENTRE, 108 Whitfield Street, W1 [387 – 4628].

The post pill generation is often surprised to learn that the first birth control clinic in this country was opened in Holloway by Marie Stopes as early as 1921.

Birth control advice is given to anyone over the age of 16, married or unmarried. It is necessary to write or phone for an appointment. A yearly fee of £3 is charged and they like a deposit of £1 and written confirmation of the appointment.

Vasectomy (male sterilization) is also available and the fee is £15. The same appointment procedure applies. They also do pregnancy testing which costs £1·50. Call any time between 10.30 a.m. and 4.30 p.m. preferably with a urine sample taken that morning.

For those faced with an unwanted pregnancy they also have an advisory service; and specially trained doctors give advice to men and women with sexual and marital difficulties.

Pregnancy testing

The Family Planning Association and the Marie Stopes Clinic (see p. 154) both do pregnancy testing and are able to give on-the-spot advice if a test proves positive. There's no such thing (as yet at any rate) as a morning-after test. The best time to be tested is when a period is a fortnight overdue. Anything earlier than this is unreliable. The procedure is that you take a urine sample, preferably taken first thing in the morning, making sure that the container is absolutely clean. Even the tiniest trace of detergent can make a positive case appear negative.

There are many private commercial pregnancy testing services which advertise, but one has to be wary since there are no regulations whatsoever regarding the qualifications of the people running these. The following are services run by reputable laboratories as recommended by *Which?*

BELMONT LABORATORIES, 188 Brent Crescent, NW10 [965 – 1477].

DELTA LABORATORIES, 44 Lupus Street, W1 [828 – 2811].

HALDANE LABORATORIES, Haldane Place, SW18 [874 – 4208].

All these laboratories will send a container and explanatory leaflet on request. The fee is £2–£3. All operate a postal service and a telephone service or you can get the result while you wait if calling personally.

Pregnancy testing is also done through some retail chemists. Some advertise this service by a sticker on the door or window. Others may operate a service but don't advertise it outside. The fee is usually £2 and the result can be sent either to your own address or to the chemist.

Abortion

Abortion isn't readily available on demand and it's important to realize this. The consent of two doctors is necessary and there must be adequate grounds for termination. Defining these adequate grounds isn't easy. Some of the clauses in the Abortion Act are open to widely varying interpretations. The risk to mental health is one of the controversial clauses and so is the social clause whereby a doctor may take into account 'the patient's actual and foreseeable environment'. Some doctors would consider the case of a single girl in the middle of a university course as having adequate grounds. Other doctors have refused to help distraught married women with large families living in appalling housing conditions.

As soon as you know you are pregnant, go to a doctor. Tell him all the circumstances and difficulties which a pregnancy will create. If he will not help you, he should tell you why. If abortion is against his conscience then he should refer you to another doctor. Sometimes a doctor may not be unsympathetic; it may be that he is unable to help you get an NHS abortion because all the available hospital beds in that area are full. In which case, he will probably refer you to the Pregnancy Advisory Service.

THE PREGNANCY ADVISORY SERVICE, 40 Margaret Street, W1 [629 – 9575].

This is a registered charity formed to ensure that the Abortion Act, 1967, works satisfactorily.

The PAS aims to help those people whose doctors are unable or unwilling to do so. Unfortunately anyone not normally resident in the UK cannot be seen. You can, if necessary, approach them direct. The PAS stress that they can't guarantee an abortion. NHS facilities are limited and private facilities, which are equally legal, can cost anything up to £100. A social worker at the PAS will discuss the problem with you and their doctors will decide whether or not there are adequate grounds for abortion. If so, they will make the necessary arrangements for a hospital or private bed. They do however stress that a girl should not be doctorless when she returns home, and for this reason insist that the GP knows the background circumstances before the girl is given an appointment. In some instances the GP may offer to help; but in any event he must be informed in case of complications afterwards.

MARIE STOPES MEMORIAL CENTRE, 108 Whitfield Street, W1 [387 – 4628].

An advisory service is available for those faced with an unwanted pregnancy.

The most common method used for terminating a pregnancy is a D and C (dilation and curettage), whereby the foetus is removed and the womb gently scraped to remove all traces of the pregnancy. Suction is an alternative method for a pregnancy under three months. A general anaesthetic is usual in both cases. For pregnancies of more than three months, an operation involving abdominal section may be necessary. This is a more complicated operation which leaves a scar and will cost around £200. Recovery time is obviously longer.

Medically speaking the earlier an abortion is carried out the better, but this does mean that a girl has to decide to act quickly. Abortion isn't always the long-term answer for the individual, though it might seem a tidy solution to an awkward predicament at the time. Sometimes girls who have an abortion find themselves in the same situation again, just as girls who have their babies adopted quickly, can get pregnant again shortly afterwards. Both are situations where emotional acceptance and adjustment are necessary afterwards. A counselling service may help or a GP should be able to arrange psychotherapy if necessary.

Having a baby

NATIONAL COUNCIL FOR THE UNMARRIED MOTHER AND HER CHILD, 255 Kentish Town Road, NW5 [267 – 1361].

The Council will put you in touch with a local social worker who can advise you about making arrangements for the birth. This social worker will probably be employed by a local authority welfare department or one of the church-based agencies, not by the National Council itself who act in this respect as a referral agency. Don't be put off by the ghastly title of Moral Welfare Officer. Most social workers *and* the National Council hate the term and wish it could be changed.

Your baby will probably be born in hospital, so you will have to book a bed and attend sessions at the ante-natal clinic beforehand. If accommodation is a problem, the social worker can arrange for you to stay in a mother-and-baby home for anything up to six weeks before and six weeks after the birth. She can also advise you about an affiliation order (see p. 159) and adoption procedure if you want this, as well as how to claim Maternity or Supplementary Benefit.

If you keep your baby, the main difficulties will be finding a job, accommodation, and a place for the baby in a day nursery or with a child-minder, all in the same area. The National Council can't necessarily provide accommodation but sometimes they may be able to help. Day nurseries are run by local authority social services departments, but, as demand far exceeds the places available, they have to give priority to the people most in need of this service, and cases are periodically reviewed. You will have to fill in an application form giving details of your circumstances. Social services departments also keep a list of registered child-minders. (Anyone who looks after a child for more than two hours at a stretch for money is required to register with the local authority so that high standards are maintained.) They also keep a list of privately run nurseries. One or two boroughs will help mothers to meet the cost of a child-minder or a private nursery if they have not been able to offer a place in a local authority day nursery.

If you are in the middle of, or just starting, a course of further education, it's important to carry on with this if possible. The more qualified you are, the more financially secure you and your child will be in the future. If you're still at school, the matter of further education, including a possible transfer to a technical college to complete A levels can be discussed at your local divisional education office whose address will be listed in the phone book, under Inner London Education Authority or under the name of your Outer London borough.

Students on grants are not normally eligible for Supplementary Benefit. You may however make an application at your local office for support for your child. The Supplementary Benefits Commission also have discretionary powers to give financial assistance to an unsupported mother in need, in order to purchase a pram and a cot, or to acquire a few basic essentials to set up home. They are not likely to offer this help unless you request it, and you may need the support of a social worker or the National Council to back your request.

Unmarried fathers

Not all unmarried fathers are irresponsible. Many fathers-to-be are deeply distressed and concerned about the future of their child and the mother. Some do in fact contact the National Council for the Unmarried Mother and her Child or the social worker concerned, to see what they can do to help. Often a girl doesn't take out an affiliation order, proving paternity, because of the unpleasantness of the procedure which involves appearing in court like a criminal, which can frequently be the kiss of death to any existing relationship. When a man wants to help financially an alternative arrangement to an affiliation order, and one which has the same legal validity, is the Form of Private Agreement, which can be for a mutually agreed amount of money, however small. A copy of this form, which has to be signed in the presence of a solicitor, can be obtained (price 12½p) from the National Council for the Unmarried Mother and her Child, 255 Kentish Town Road, NW5.

Because so many of the social workers involved in helping unsupported mothers are themselves female, it's easy for a man to feel that they're automatically 'on the girl's side'. Most enlightened social workers welcome and encourage the emotional support which the father can give, particularly at a time when a girl feels vulnerable. Most mother-and-baby homes welcome visits from the father. A shot-gun wedding, which used to be a common solution, isn't to be recommended; not without a lot of thought. Getting *un*married is a much more difficult business. You may need the help of a social worker to convince parents of this.

THE FAMILY SERVICE AND INQUIRY DEPARTMENT of the Salvation Army, 280 Mare Street, E8 [985 – 1181].

Help is given in tracing missing fathers, married or otherwise, for whom the social pressures have been too much. Some men find it easier to talk to another man about their personal problems than to a female social worker. The Salvation Army *won't* reveal addresses, they *will* respect the confidence of both parties. They act as a go-between in times of illness or distress, and will forward postal or money orders.

Venereal disease

Venereal Disease is the collective term given to a whole group of sexually transmitted infections, gonorrhoea and syphilis being the most commonly known. The huge increase in VD over recent years is due to a number of reasons, sexual permissiveness being only one. Greater social mobility is a contributory factor; holidays abroad and air travel for example mean a wider and quicker spread of infection. The female contraceptive pill doesn't provide the same protection as the male sheath and the germs themselves are becoming more resistant to antibiotics.

An estimated one in 300 people visit VD or Special Clinics in Britain each year, the larger percentage of these being in the 16–30 age group. Not all the people visiting a clinic will have necessarily caught an infection, but it's always better to go for a check-up than to worry. Girls can be infected and yet show no obvious symptoms. Homosexuals can pass on VD to each other. VD makes no difference to a pregnancy and provided that treatment is obtained in good time the baby will be all right. Long-term untreated VD can however mean that a girl may later be unable to have a baby. Some books on VD include *So Now You Know about VD*, a Family Doctor booklet (12½p) available from Family Doctor House, 47–51 Chalton Street, NW1; *First Report* by a doctor, published by *The Diary*, 16 Molton Street, W1 which will be sent in a plain wrapper (price 17½p); *Venereal Diseases* by R. S. Morton, Pelican (17½p) and *The Venereal Diseases* by Dr R. D. Catterall, an Impact paperback published by Evans (37½p).

VD CLINICS. You don't need a doctor's note to attend a so-called Special Clinic. You don't usually need an appointment, but some hospitals are now starting this system in their clinics. Unlike many out-patient clinics, they do make a positive effort to see people as soon as possible after they arrive. There is usually a social worker attached to the clinic and you will probably be asked to suggest that your partner goes along for a check-up too. If you're reluctant to do this yourself, the social worker will take on this follow-up call. It will be done tactfully and no compulsion is involved whatsoever. Many steady couples come along to the clinic together and there are separate departments for men and women. Here is a list of clinics in the London area which open from 10 a.m. to 7 p.m. each weekday, including lunch-hours and Saturday mornings. It helps the staff if new patients don't come too near closing time.

Hammersmith, MARTHA AND LUKE CLINIC, West London Hospital, Hammersmith Road, W6 [748 – 3441].

Lambeth, LYDIA DEPARTMENT, St Thomas's Hospital, Lambeth Palace Road, SE1 [928 – 9292].

Paddington, SPECIAL CLINIC, St Mary's Hospital, Norfolk Place, W2 [262 – 1280].

Southwark, SPECIAL CLINIC, Guy's Hospital, St Thomas Street, SE1 [407 – 7600].

W1, JAMES PRINGLE HOUSE, Middlesex Hospital, James

Pringle Street, Charlotte Street, W1 [636 – 8333. Ring for appointment].

There are, of course, other Special Clinics in other hospitals all over London but with shorter sessions and at different times for men and women. For further information there is a special exclusive direct-line VD telephone service run by the City of Westminster. Phone 928 – 3401 and they will tell you the address of your nearest clinic and the next session. They will also send on request explanatory leaflets through the post. Some people prefer to collect these direct from the reception desk at City Hall, Victoria Street, SW1 where they will be kept for you in a plain envelope.

ARREST

If you are arrested, the police must tell you what offence you are charged with. They should allow you to telephone your family, solicitor or a friend at the earliest possible opportunity. The police cannot compel you to accompany them to the police station unless you have been arrested, although in practice it is usually better to go quietly if asked. A refusal can easily lead to a scuffle if tempers get frayed and you may then find yourself being charged with resisting arrest. You cannot be compelled to answer questions, make or sign a statement and you should not be pressurized or persuaded into doing so. It is advisable to state 'I do not wish to say anything until I have seen my solicitor', rather than to remain silent.

NATIONAL COUNCIL FOR CIVIL LIBERTIES, 152 Camden High Street, NW1 [485 – 9497].

NCCL will investigate and take up cases on behalf of individuals and is particularly concerned about citizens' rights as they affect young people, for example the withholding of grants by local authorities from students who demonstrate, and the arbitrary police powers of search under the Dangerous Drugs Act which means that anyone with long hair and way-out clothes is liable to be stopped and searched in the street for drugs on those grounds alone.

They publish a variety of booklets including *Arrest: A Guide to Citizens' Rights* (7½p), as well as a *Handbook of Citizens' Rights* (25p).

They also issue a pocket-sized printed card to all members of NCCL, on what to do if arrested.

LEGAL AID AND ADVICE

Citizens' Advice Bureau

If you need a solicitor for any reason, go to a branch of the Citizens' Advice Bureau. All branches of the CAB, which are given in the phone book, keep a list of solicitors who operate the Legal Aid and Advice Scheme. There are two advice schemes, statutory and voluntary and which you choose depends on your financial circumstances. The most you can be asked to pay is £1 for a half-hour interview under the Voluntary Scheme, which will cover most problems. Legal Aid is available to help you bring or defend proceedings in court. A CAB solicitor will advise you on how to make an application.

CABs tackle a multitude of practical problems on behalf of their callers. They will always explain current legislation in terms of the individual concerned. They give advice on what to do about consumer complaints, landlord and tenant disputes, income tax, problems of immigrants, etc., etc., etc. They keep a stack of leaflets on a variety of subjects. You don't need an appointment, just walk in. Some CABs have evening sessions but check the hours by phone first.

Race Relations

The Race Relations Act exists to stop discrimination by colour or race in the fields of housing, education and employment. It covers services and facilities such as banking and insurance, grants and loans, places of entertainment, hotels and transport. A leaflet (price 2½p) outlining the Act can be obtained from HMSO or from a CAB.

Complaints under the Act should be submitted within a two-month period to: Room 151, Fourth Floor, Greater London Conciliation Committee, Palace Chambers, Bridge Street, SW1.

ADVISE, 283 Gray's Inn Road, WC1. [Emergency 24-hour number 278 – 1487; office number 278 – 5614].

Advise is a 24-hour immigrant advice centre providing a free legal service to the Black community of London. Like Release, and the National Council for Civil Liberties, they have a printed card setting out one's basic rights if arrested.

As Advise deal with a variety of problems confronting the immigrant, they also need all sorts of volunteer help. Ring, write or call.

INTERNATIONAL PERSONNEL, 4a Balham Station Road, SW12 [675 – 0941], is the first of what is hoped will be a national network of employment agencies supported by the Martin Luther King Foundation. Their aim is to find better jobs which match people's abilities, and they cover all types of employment.

8

GETTING AWAY

Sometimes you will want to get out of London – for weekends, for holidays, for some special event, just to get away. You may want to get off on your own or be with other people. Either way there is a variety of organizations which can help you. Each person may want something different, but the same organization may be able to help a wide variety of people. Most of these organizations are listed alphabetically in this chapter, but others (where their primary function is not to help would-be travellers) appear in other parts of the book. Use this table to find the organization which you think may help you.

At weekends

Holidays in Britain

Holidays abroad

Adventure holidays

Hobby holidays

Outdoor holidays

Study holidays

Working holidays

BRITISH RAIL TRAVEL CENTRE, 12 Lower Regent Street, SW1.

This is a booking and inquiry centre for all British Rail services including rail-and-sea journeys to Ireland and the Continent. They will deal only with personal callers. The main-line rail terminal inquiries are listed in the London telephone directory, under British Rail, by areas. This includes Motorail Services, Car-Ferry Services and hotel reservations at British Transport hotels.

BRITISH SCHOOLS EXPLORING SOCIETY, Temple Chambers, Temple Avenue, EC4 [353 – 2100].

Each year the Society organizes arduous expeditions in Britain and abroad for about seventy-five young men between the ages of $16\frac{1}{2}$ and 19. You need not still be at school. You must apply in the autumn before the year in which you want to go, preferably through your school, firm or club. You must be physically fit and able to swim. The cost of the expeditions, which last five to six weeks, is about £150, but some part-scholarships are available.

BRITISH TOURIST AUTHORITY, 64 St James's Street, SW1 [629 – 9191].

The BTA is the statutory authority for promoting tourism in Britain. It is not a travel agency but an information centre with a wealth of information for personal callers. The BTA publishes lists of the principal events in Britain including exhibitions, concerts, traditional customs, sports events, and miscellaneous events such as the National Ploughing Match, brass band festivals and traction engine rallies. It also has lists of holidays suitable for young and old people (including pensioners), pony-trekking and riding holidays, centres for boating holidays, camping and caravan sites, farmhouse accommodation, excursions in and around London, hotels with fishing facilities and haunted houses. In addition, it has a list of visits to factories with opening times and details about arranging visits. The list includes such things as the Nuffield Radio Astronomy Laboratories at Jodrell Bank, Scotch whisky distillers, brewers, manufacturers of pottery and bone china, electrical engineers, food and beverage manufacturers, newspapers, Post Office services, shipbuilders, textile manufacturers and water boards. The BTA publishes a guide to London, *This Month in London.* These lists can be obtained at the BTA offices, or through bookshops, or the Government Bookshop, 49 High Holborn, WC1.

BRITISH WATERWAYS BOARD, Delamere Terrace, W2 [286 – 6101].

The canals of Britain offer over 1,000 miles of inland cruising. The Board is responsible for the licensing of private vessels and moorings (Pleasure Craft Licensing Office, Willow Grange, Church Road, Watford WD1 3QA). Cruisers are available for hire from the Board (Nantwich Pleasure Craft Base, Chester Road, Nantwich, Cheshire). The Board provides lists of area waterway information, including where to buy a boat, arrangements for mooring a boat in London, cruising clubs, addresses of hire firms and firms organizing canal trips.

The London Zoo Waterbus summer service from Little Venice (Blomfield Road, W2, near Warwick Avenue underground station) to the Zoo leaves every hour on the hour on weekdays and Sunday afternoons. The 'Jenny Wren' runs along the Regent's Canal between Camden Town and Little Venice and returns, a journey of about ninety minutes. (Further information from 485 – 6210.) These boats and the privately owned 'Jason' [286 – 3428] can be booked for private parties. A new boat, 'Lady of Regents', is specially designed to cater for receptions, conferences, cocktail parties and small functions (forty people maximum) of all kinds. She can be chartered for half or whole days or evenings and catering is provided to meet individual customers' requirements.

The Waterways Museum (Stoke Bruerne, near Towcester, Northants) can be reached either from the Grand Union Canal or from the M1 or A5. It records the history of the two centuries of British inland waterways.

BUSES AND COACHES.

Green Line coaches operate within a radius of about thirty miles from central London. Travel information from 222 – 1234.

Eastern National Coach Station, 250 Pentonville Road, N1 [278 – 6902]. Services to East Anglia including Southend and Stansted airports and Tilbury and Harwich.

King's Cross Coach Station, 15–25 Caledonia Street, N1 [837 – 7373]. Services to the North and various British and Continental tours.

Victoria Coach Station, 164 Buckingham Palace Road, SW1 [730 – 0202]. Services all over Britain operated by the main provincial coach companies.

London Transport and Green Line issue Red Rover and Green Rover tickets, which give you unlimited mileage during a given period.

CAMPING CLUB OF GREAT BRITAIN, 11 Lower Grosvenor Place, SW1 [828 – 9232].

Membership of the Camping Club entitles you to a list of camp sites in Britain, access to forty Club-operated sites and the use of an all-in foreign touring service, and their monthly magazine giving information and ideas on camping holidays. The different units of the Club organize regular activities and rallies all over the country. There are also specialist sections for caravan owners, motor caravanners, trailer tents, canoeists, lightweight campers, photographers, mountaineers and people interested in folk dance and song. The Club publishes an annual booklet, *International Camping*, and the Social and Cultural section organizes holidays on the continent and charter flights further afield.

CAREERS RESEARCH AND ADVISORY CENTRE, Bateman Street, Cambridge.

CRAC have published a pamphlet *While you Wait*, a guide to opportunities between school and university for further education. It is presented free with the compliments of Barclays Bank. The sections cover voluntary service, teaching, office work, secretarial and other study courses in Britain and abroad. It lists agencies organizing *au pair* and paying-guest arrangements.

CAR FERRIES.

On most car ferries you can take your car to the continent free for short trips (four and five days) if four adults (two children count as one adult) are travelling. The length of the trip includes both the day of departure and the day of return. Weekend bookings must be for Thursday to the continent and for Monday homeward. Car ferry companies often have arrangements for hiring camping equipment and car trailers and may provide other services such as meal packs and discounts at hotels.

CENTRAL BUREAU FOR EDUCATIONAL VISITS AND EXCHANGES, 91 Victoria Street, SW1 [799 – 3941].

The Bureau is the national office for information and advice on all forms of educational exchanges and travel for young people. It publishes the following three annual booklets each covering a special subject and listing organizations which arrange individual exchanges or cheap travel facilities. Self-addressed stamped envelopes (9 by 5 ins.) should accompany requests for any of these publications. They cost 20p each.

Working Holidays & Voluntary Service Abroad covers traineeships, farm work, English teaching, work in youth hostels, etc. There are very few opportunities for anyone under 18. The booklet also lists organizations which arrange for *au pair* posts abroad, and lists over 100 agencies in Britain, Europe and elsewhere which run a wide variety of projects.

Youth Visits Abroad lists nearly 300 holidays with addresses of the organizing agencies. A short selection from one year's list includes: mountain walking in the Pyrénées, language courses, winter sports, canoeing and camping in the Black Forest, staying with a family in Bulgaria, reindeer drives with Lapp families in Finland, drama and music festivals, archaeology courses and excavations, pony-trekking in Iceland, visiting a kibbutz in Israel, cycling in Italy, fine art courses in Holland, camping in Russia.

Vacation Courses Abroad lists more obviously educational holidays, although a certain number of riding, sailing and ski-ing courses are included.

In addition, the Bureau produces *Young Visitors to Britain* (10p post free) which lists many forms of holiday and summer course in Britain, and gives details of accommodation and exchange organizations.

COMMON COLD RESEARCH UNIT, Harvard Hospital, Coombe Road, Salisbury, Wiltshire [Salisbury 22485].

Volunteer helpers are often required for research into the common cold and related illnesses. They must be between 18 and 50 years of age and are required to spend ten days at the Unit. They are isolated in pairs or threes, and friends can come together, although partners may be found for single volunteers who will have separate bedrooms.

The Unit has very comfortable accommodation overlooking beautiful country, ideal for walking. The food is reputedly good and indoor and outdoor games are available. There is a library and newspapers of the volunteers' choice are provided. There is plenty of time for study, open-air recreation and relaxation. Return fares and 35p per day pocket money are paid to volunteers.

The research procedures are simple and, according to the Unit, 'not at all traumatic'. Often only one third of those attending get even mild colds.

Further particulars can be found in most public libraries in Greater London, or can be had from the Hospital, who welcome inquiries.

COMMONWEALTH YOUTH EXCHANGE COUNCIL, 18 Northumberland Avenue, W C2 [930 – 1763].

The Council, representative of the major bodies active in the field of Commonwealth youth exchange and supported by British Council funds, will advise local authorities, businesses, teachers, youth leaders, and young people themselves, on ways to establish and develop closer youth contact between Britain and other Commonwealth countries.

This contact takes the form of school or youth association links, the dissemination of information, and cheap travel exchange between Britain and other Commonwealth countries of groups with common interests.

COMMUNITY EDUCATION FOR YOUNG EUROPEANS, King's Cross Training Centre, Crestfield Street, W C1 [837 – 0789].

The CEYE runs a programme of international exchange combining community service with further education in Europe. The programme is open to all young adults aged between 17 and 25 irrespective of educational or language qualifications.

The community service consists mainly of acting as nursing auxiliaries in mental, geriatric and general hospitals. This is combined with a study programme into European political, economic, social and cultural activities, and assistance with gaining proficiency in the language. The educational programme is designed to cater for all young adults and CEYE is eager to attract 'non-academic' participants. There is a programme fee of £120, but CEYE will advise you on how this money may be raised.

The minimum period of service is twelve months (usually starting in late August) and you are provided with your return fare, pocket money, full board and accommodation. There are also study courses in the evenings and special residential courses.

CONCORDIA (YOUTH SERVICE VOLUNTEERS), 11a Albemarle Street, W1 [629 – 3367].

Concordia organizes international work camps in Britain and sends British volunteers to youth camps in Europe. Work in British camps consists mainly of fruit-picking for piece-work rates, and a board and lodging fee is charged. Most European camps engage in voluntary work, from forestry and reconstruction to social work, and there are camps for archaeological students in Italy and Spain. In all European camps board and lodging is free, but wages are not paid, except at the camps helping with the French wine harvest in October. In all cases volunteers pay their own travel expenses. Applicants for British camps should be aged between 16 and 30, and for European camps between 18 and 25, although there are a few vacancies for 16- and 17-year-olds. Detailed information about British camps is available from January and for European camps from May. A stamped addressed envelope should be sent with all inquiries.

COUNTRYSIDE COMMISSION, 1 Cambridge Gate, W1 [935 – 5533].

There are ten National Parks in England and Wales covering 5,258 square miles of varied countryside including Snowdonia, the Pembrokeshire coast, the Brecon Beacons, Exmoor, Dartmoor, Northumberland, the Lake District, the Yorkshire Dales, the North York Moors and the Peak District. The National Parks are not on the whole publicly owned, but the Commission is responsible for 'preserving and enhancing their natural beauty and promoting their enjoyment by the public'. Local planning authorities, one for each park, operate warden and information services, and provide such facilities as camping and caravanning sites, accommodation and parking.

CRUSE, 6 Lion Gate Gardens, Richmond, Surrey.

Cruse is an organization to link and advise widows. It publishes a list of holiday organizations, summer schools and school holiday activities.

Embassies and National Tourist Offices

Many embassies in London publish lists of study, camping, sporting and other holidays in their own country and many countries have national tourist offices in London, which supply information about the regions, seasonal events and travel facilities in their country. For instance, the French Tourist Office in Piccadilly has a booklet on *Holidays for the Under-Thirties in France* and information on camping in France.

Here are the addresses of some countries' tourist offices:

Austrian State Tourist Department, 16 Conduit Street, W1.
Belgian National Tourist Office, 66 Haymarket, SW1.
Cyprus Trade and Tourist Centre, 213 Regent Street, W1.
Czechoslovak Travel Bureau, 45 Oxford Street, W1.
Danish Tourist Board, 169 Regent Street, W1.
Finnish Travel Information Centre, 56 Haymarket, SW1.
French Government Tourist Office, 178 Piccadilly, W1.
German National Tourist Office, 67 Conduit Street, W1.
Irish Tourist Office, 150 New Bond Street, W1.
Israel Government Tourist Office, 59 St James's Street, SW1.
Italian State Tourist Office, 201 Regent Street, W1.
Malta Government Tourist Office, 24 Haymarket, W1.
Moroccan Tourist Office, 174 Regent Street, W1.
Netherlands Tourist Office, 38 Hyde Park Gate, SW7.
Norwegian National Tourist Office, 20 Pall Mall, SW1.
Portuguese State Tourist and Trade Information Office, 20 Lower Regent Street, SW1.
Romanian National Tourist Office, 98–9 Jermyn Street, SW1.
Soviet Travel Agency, 292 Regent Street, SW1.
Spanish National Tourist Office, 70 Jermyn Street, SW1.
Swedish Travel Association, 52–3 Conduit Street, W1.
Swiss National Tourist Office, 1 New Coventry Street, W1.
Tunisian Tourist Centre, 50 Conduit Street, W1.
Turkish Tourism Information Office, 49 Conduit Street, SW1.
Yugoslav National Tourist Office, 143 Regent Street, W1.

FARM CAMPS.

There are a number of farm work camps in this country for 16–30-year-olds which help farmers with fruit-picking, harvesting and other seasonal work. You pay for travel, board and lodging, and earn money by working. Most work camps recruit internationally. The Ministry of Agriculture (Great Westminster

House, Horseferry Road, SW1 [834 – 8511]) will supply a list of organizations to which you can apply and the Central Bureau for Educational Visits and Exchanges lists some farm camps abroad.

FORESTRY COMMISSION, 25 Savile Row, W1 [734 – 0221].

The Commission has a pamphlet listing the principal facilities in forests throughout the country. These include forest walks, nature trails (see p. 179), picnic and camping sites. Some forests near London are: Maulden Wood, Ampthill; Queen Wood near Watlington; Halton Wood near Wendover; Branshill near Camberley; Potterscrough Wood near St Albans; Bedgebury near Hawkhurst (the National Pinetum); Joydens Wood, Bexley; Abinger near Dorking; St Leonard's Forest near Horsham. All forests have wardens who can advise on the use of the forest.

HOME INTERCHANGE LTD, 19 Bolton Street, W1 [629 – 1555 and 789 – 2733].

Home Interchange publishes an annual directory of houses available for exchange both in Britain and abroad, with a particularly wide selection in the United States. The charge for listing your house or flat in the directory is approximately £4, and information for entry should be submitted (on the form available from Home Interchange Ltd) in January, or in February and March for entry in its supplements. You will then receive a copy of the directory and its supplements, through which you then arrange your own exchange.

INOCULATIONS AND VACCINATION.

When travelling abroad, particularly outside Europe, you may need certain immunization certificates. The embassy of the country concerned will advise if you are in doubt. You can arrange injections with your own doctor; some are free under the NHS, but some he may charge you for. Even under the NHS he can charge you for the International Certificate of Vaccination. You will then have to have the Certificate stamped by the local Medical Officer of Health.

The Department of Health (Elephant and Castle, SE1 [407 – 5522]) issues a list of vaccination clinics and the following clinics will immunize and issue certificates if you have an appointment: BOAC Airways Terminal Medical Department,

SW1 [834 – 2323]; Hospital for Tropical Diseases, 4 St Pancras Way, NW1 [387 – 4411]; Vaccinating Centre, 53 Great Cumberland Place, W1 [262 – 6456]. The Casualty Department of Charing Cross Hospital, Agar Street, Strand, WC2 will immunize you without an appointment at any time of the day and night. All clinics charge about £1 for this service.

KIBBUTZ REPRESENTATIVE, 4–12 Regent Street, SW1 [930 – 5152, Extension 333].

A kibbutz is a communal society in Israel, in which all the means of production are owned by the community as a whole. There are two kibbutz schemes: one for the potential settler in Israel and one for the working visitor. For the working visitor scheme you must be between 18 and 35, have a return ticket or adequate funds for the return journey, and be prepared to work seven or eight hours a day for six days a week. The minimum stay on a kibbutz is one month as it is not considered that a shorter stay would enable the visitor to benefit from or understand the way of life. The work is mainly of an agricultural nature, but some is involved with industry. Visitors may also be required to help in the kitchen or laundry.

No wages are paid, but all needs are supplied regardless of the kind of work you do. The organizers point out that the work can be tedious, unpleasant and dirty and you must have the willpower, stamina, and feeling of commitment to meet the challenge of a different society.

LONDON TRANSPORT ENQUIRY OFFICES, 55 Broadway, SW1 [222 – 1234]; also at Piccadilly Circus, Oxford Circus, Euston, King's Cross and Victoria underground stations.

London Transport publish a number of information booklets about London and its environs. Relevant to this chapter are *Country Walks* (25p each), a series which carefully describes walks around London's countryside with photographs, Ordnance Survey maps, notes on places of interest and travel instructions; and the *Day Out* leaflets (free) which describe a day's outing to a particular area, such as Richmond or Epping Forest.

Red Bus Rover tickets give you a day's unlimited travel over 1,500 miles of Red central bus routes. You can buy them at most underground stations and bus garages. These tickets may not be used on the Underground and are valid after 9.30 a.m. Mondays to Fridays, and all day on Saturdays, Sundays and Bank Holidays (40p adults, 20p children under 14).

NATIONAL GARDENS SCHEME, 57 Lower Belgrave Square, SW1 [730 – 0355].

The National Gardens Scheme publishes an annual booklet listing well over 1,000 private gardens in England and Wales which are open to the public. The money raised on entry charges goes to the Queen's Institute of District Nursing and the National Trust.

MINISTRY OF PUBLIC BUILDING AND WORKS, Lambeth Bridge House, SE1 [735 – 7611].

This Ministry is responsible for preserving and presenting to the public many of the ancient historic sites and buildings of Britain. Admission to the sites may be free or within the price range of 1 to 12p. For 75p a year you can get a 'Season Ticket to History' (half-price for children and pensioners) which admits you free. A list of monuments is supplied with the season ticket.

The sites near London include Houghton House, Ampthill (reputedly Bunyan's 'House Beautiful'); Audley End Mansion, Saffron Walden; Lullingstone Roman Villa near Tonbridge; Dover Castle and Pevensey Castle in Sussex.

NATIONAL TRUST, 42 Queen Anne's Gate, SW1 [930 – 1841].

The National Trust for Places of Historic Interest or Natural Beauty helps to preserve the best of the countryside and our finest buildings. You may join the Trust as an individual member or by corporate membership through school, college, youth club, etc. Ordinary members, £2 per year; other members of the family living at the same address, £1 per year. Life members pay £50 and life membership cards admit two people to National Trust properties. Junior membership (for those under 21) is only 50p a year if you belong to a group (such as the Scout and Guide Associations, YHA, etc.) which is already a corporate member of the Trust. Membership gives you free access to some 200 Trust properties where there are entry fees for the general public.

National Trust properties near London include Winston

Churchill's former home Chartwell, near Westerham in Kent; Knole, one of the largest houses in England, built between 1456 and 1603, near Sevenoaks in Kent; Sissinghurst Castle with the famous gardens created by the late Victoria Sackville-West and her husband Sir Harold Nicolson, near Cranbrook; Ham House, a perfect example of Stewart domestic architecture, at Richmond; Polesden Lacey, a graceful Regency villa in delightful surroundings, near Dorking; Batemans, the seventeenth-century house where Rudyard Kipling lived for over thirty years, near Burwash in Sussex; Bodiam Castle, the ruin of a moated medieval castle, near Hawkhurst; Petworth, with its magnificent collection of paintings by Van Dyck and Turner, on the A 286 to Chichester; Hughenden Manor, Disraeli's home, near High Wycombe; West Wycombe Park, the Palladian house in beautiful grounds, in Buckinghamshire; Cliveden, with its sweeping views of the Thames, near Maidenhead; and in London itself, the George Inn, at Southwark, the only remaining galleried inn in London, which is still used as a pub, and Osterley Park, the Elizabethan house remodelled by Robert Adam.

The National Trust owns and maintains not only houses but also open countryside. Among these properties are Blackdown, 600 acres of woods and downs, near Haslemere; Sheffield Park Gardens, 140 acres of gardens laid out by Capability Brown in 1775, midway between East Grinstead and Lewes; Runnymede, the meadows where King John signed Magna Carta; Box Hill, 800 acres of chalk downlands and woods, near Dorking; Hatfield Forest of over 1,000 acres, near Bishop's Stortford; Finchampstead Ridges, 100 acres of heath and woodland, near Crowthorne in Berkshire, and Ashridge Estate, covering six square miles along the Chilterns, near Berkhamsted.

The National Trust runs two-week spring and summer work camps (Acorn Camps) where volunteers (from 16 for men, from 17 for girls) work to improve the Trust's properties. A typical summer programme would include projects such as making access paths and a camp site in Westmorland; restoring a canal tow-path in Warwickshire; removing ugly fence posts on an Anglesey headland; landscaping a garden in Northern Ireland. You pay travel expenses and a small contribution for board and lodging, which may be in a cottage or a castle, or under canvas.

The Trust also has a list of camping and caravanning sites on its properties.

NATIONAL UNION OF STUDENTS, Travel Service, Clifton House, 10–12 Euston Road, NW1 [387 – 9456].

You can join the NUS as a sixth-form Associate Member at 15 as long as you are still being educated full-time. Any student can use the NUS Travel Service except for the student charter flights, which are restricted to full-time students. The NUS organizes month-long language courses, placements on work projects abroad and a great variety of other holidays and cheap travel facilities. As a student you have the right to an International Student Identity Card for reduced entry to exhibitions, museums and student accommodation and restaurants on the Continent.

The National Union of Students, Vacation Work Department, 3 Endsleigh Street, WC1 advertises vacation jobs through fortnightly college bulletins. These are not sent to individuals but jobs in the London area are given in a daily bulletin which can be seen at the office during working hours.

NATURE TRAILS.

A nature trail is a signposted walk especially devised to show the animals, birds, plants, trees and other points of interest in the area. The British Tourist Authority has a list of trails (10p) telling you where information about them is available. Nature trails near London are at Sandy, Bedfordshire; Finchampstead Ridges, Berkshire; Coombe Hill, Wendover; Fingringhoe Nature Reserve, Essex; Hothfield Common near Ashford, Kent; Chinnor Hill, Oxfordshire; Barfold Copse Reserve near Haslemere. There is a children's indoor nature trail at the Natural History Museum in Cromwell Road, SW7, based on the collections. Trail sheets are available at the Children's Centre in the museum from 10.30 a.m. to 4.30 p.m. on Saturdays and during school holidays.

OUTWARD BOUND TRUST, Iddesleigh House, Caxton Street, SW1 [222 – 2926].

The Trust arranges twenty-six-day training courses using the challenges of the sea and mountains to enable young people to establish self-confidence and bring out their latent qualities of leadership. The courses are run for young people aged 14–20.

PASSPORT OFFICE, Clive House, Petty France, SW1 [222 – 8010].

Three weeks should be allowed to obtain a passport or any other passport service, although there are arrangements for the speedy treatment of cases of genuine emergency. Passports can be obtained through local Employment Exchanges or by post or personal application from the Passport Office, which is open Monday to Friday from 9 a.m. to 4.30 p.m., and for emergencies (serious illness or urgent business, but *not* holiday travel) for a further two hours daily and between 10 a.m. and 12 noon on Saturdays, Sundays and Public Holidays (except Christmas Day). Passports are issued for ten years and are not renewable. The fee is £5.

The orange British Visitor's passport which is valid for one year only for holiday travel to a limited number of countries can be obtained only by personal application at an Employment Exchange. The fee is £1·50.

In summer it is wise to apply nine weeks before you travel.

Summer Schools and Weekend Courses

There are a large number of organizations, cultural, political, educational, which organize one or more weekend or 'summer' schools a year, some of the schools being held at Easter. The standard of accommodation varies and with it the price. The cheapest are about £12 per week, but some specialized courses may cost as much as £50 per week. Some are more study-centred, others more relaxed but the important point is that you meet 'like-minded' people with the same interests and hobbies, and have the opportunity to indulge in your own special interests more than usual.

The following organizations will send information about such courses:

BRITISH COUNCIL, 2/3 Bloomsbury Square, WC1 [240 – 2468].

The Council supplies information about a large number of

summer courses for overseas visitors only – about 100 courses in English language and related subjects, and other courses in subjects mainly related to the arts.

NATIONAL INSTITUTE OF ADULT EDUCATION, 35 Queen Anne Street, W1 [580 – 3155].

The Institute publishes a six-monthly calendar, *Residential Short Courses* (15p), in March and September. Courses cover antiques, archaeology, art, canals, conservation and local studies, teachers' courses, drama, management, languages, literature, music, natural history, needlework, photography, preparation for external degrees, religion and sociology. (*See p. 133.*)

WORKERS' EDUCATIONAL ASSOCIATION, London District, 32 Tavistock Square, WC1 [387 – 8966].

WEA residential courses are related to previous study by the applicant – they are an extension of work in evening classes, offering full-time study facilities with resident tutors. (*See p. 133.*)

THAMES LAUNCHES, York Villa, Church Street, Twickenham, [892 – 9041].

During the summer months Thames Launches run day and evening services to and from Charing Cross, Westminster, Hampton Court Palace, Richmond, Kew Gardens, the Tower of London and Greenwich. Day cruises run from 10 a.m. and evening cruises from about 7.00 p.m. There are reduced rates for parties of twelve and over, and the round tours vary in length from two to ten hours. On the full-day tours lunch and tea are available, and on other cruises there is a licensed cafeteria on board.

You can hire launches for private parties of from forty to 220 passengers. All hire vessels are fully licensed and a catering service is available.

Travel Agencies

Apart from booking holidays and tours, travel agents sell train and bus tickets, book airway tickets and hotels, arrange car hire abroad and will work out itineraries.

Three travel agents which include in their programmes

something rather different from the usual sun-sea-and-a-splash-of-culture (not that we have anything against *that*, of course) are:

ERNA LOW TRAVEL SERVICE LTD, 47 Old Brompton Road, SW7 [589 – 8881].

They arrange holidays for various age groups from 8 years upwards. These included in one year riding in Denmark, canoeing in France, studying archaeology at Herculaneum, water sports in Malta, French, German and Spanish language courses, house parties in Britain and ski-ing at over 100 European centres.

COUNTRY-WIDE HOLIDAYS ASSOCIATION, Birch Heys, Cromwell Range, Manchester M14 7DJ [Rusholme 2887].

Among the 'special feature' holidays arranged one year were courses on railways, archaeology, sailing, rock climbing, music, painting, photography, field studies, bird watching and folk dancing.

HOLIDAY FELLOWSHIP LTD, 142 Great North Way, NW4 [203 – 3381].

Apart from the usual winter-sports programme, they have a variety of spring and summer holidays in Britain and abroad, for example orienteering, geology, golf, painting, photography, archaeology, bridge, dancing, music, gardening, pony-trekking, pottery and antiques.

VACATION-WORK, 9 Park End Street, Oxford.

Vacation-Work produces two annual directories (£1·12½ post free).

Summer Jobs in Britain lists employers looking for staff in factories, offices, hotels and restaurants, domestic and gardening work, language schools, voluntary service and as drivers.

Summer Jobs Abroad lists employment in similar fields all over the world – alphabetically from Andorra to Yugoslavia, geographically from Argentina to Canada. It also gives organizations arranging *au pair*, paying guest and exchange visits. There is a section on holiday and travel, giving cheap travel facilities and travel agents catering for young people.

Vacation-Work are also the UK agents for a third directory *The Summer Employment Directory of the United States* (£2 post free) which lists 80,000 vacancies including work in hotels, ranches, summer camps and national parks.

By joining Vacation-Work International (at the same address) you can get a discount on the directories, up-to-date bulletins on additional information about jobs and cheap travel facilities to some of the jobs listed in the directories. VWI also arranges working holidays in various parts of the world for members.

YOUTH HOSTELS ASSOCIATION, 29 John Adam Street, WC2 [839 – 1722].

Membership of the YHA is open to everyone of 5 years and over. The Association has over 260 hostels in England and Wales, and there are a further 150 hostels in Scotland and Ireland. Membership (over 21, £1; 16–20, 62½p; under 16, 25p) gives you access to all these, to 3,000 hostels in Europe, and to hostels in many other countries including Australia, Ceylon, Japan, Kenya and the United States.

The hostels in Britain are for those who travel 'under their own steam', cyclists, walkers, climbers, etc., although you may drive to your first hostel and leave your car there during the period of your holiday. Hostels provide dormitory accommodation, washing facilities, a common-room and a kitchen where you can cook your own food. Most hostels can also provide cooked meals. The cost of an overnight stay is 20p to 30p according to age. There are twelve hostels which provide family accommodation for families with children under 5.

The YHA handbook, which you receive on joining, gives the addresses of all hostels and other useful information. At the John Adam Street office there is a YHA shop with an excellent range of clothes and equipment for the outdoor life.

The YHA also offers a wide range of organized holidays through YHA Home Tours (8 St Stephen's Hill, St Alban's, Herts.). There are Eagle Holidays for 11–15-year-olds and for those over 16, a wide variety of holidays such as a tour of the canals in a horse-drawn narrowboat, an aqualung-diving training course, wildlife and rural crafts courses, orienteering and pony-trekking.

Local YHA groups organize regular meetings and social evenings throughout the year and there are weekend programmes at many hostels. Details of these are given in the YHA magazine, *Youth Hosteller*. Volunteer help is welcome for repairing and redecorating hostels and for other work. At Easter and in the summer the YHA needs a large number of leaders for walking and cycling holidays and instructors in sailing, rock climbing and photography. Board and lodging and fares are paid.

9

GOODS, SERVICES AND ADVICE CENTRES

If you live in London it may not be easy to find the 'little man round the corner' who can just do this or that. On the other hand there are many services which you can only find in London. Either way, how do you find them?

One good source is the London yellow pages classified telephone directory. This alphabet from the directory shows that anything is possible, whether likely or unlikely:

Abattoirs, Bingo halls, Car hire, Church furnishings, Dance halls, Embassies, Fork-lift trucks, Fuel distributors, Genealogists, Glaziers, Hay and straw merchants, Health clubs, Invisible repairers, Impresarios, Jewellers, Joiners and carpenters, Key Cutters, Laundries, Literary agents, Market Gardeners, Minicabs, Nurseries for children, Old people's homes, Pawnbrokers, Post Office services, Probation officers, Quantity surveyors, Race courses, Removal contractors, Rag merchants, Sailing instructors, Schools and colleges of all types (dancing, hairdressing, tennis, nursery or university), Social service and welfare organizations, Solicitors, Tattooists, Translators and interpreters, Upholsterers, Van hire, Window cleaners, Whisky distillers, X-ray services, Yacht chandlers and Zinc workers.

Another source of information is your local newspaper, which will certainly have a small ads. section listing such things as:

Accommodation, Builders and decorators, Car Hire, Church notices, Driving schools, Furniture removing, Guitar tuition, House exchange, Insurance brokers, Jobs, Lino laying, Missing persons, Nursery schools, Official notices, Piano tuning, Reconditioned gas cookers, Tiling and roofing experts, Upholsterers, Valuers, Wedding cars.

This section lists some of the more basic and enterprising services and centres. For a far fuller list refer to *Help Yourself in*

London by Michael Balfour, published by the Garnstone Press (90p), which lists a total of 2,610 separate organizations.

Advice Centres

If you're setting up home, London offers the chance to really look round at what's available on the market so you can get the best possible value for money. When shopping around be careful about the word 'Centre'. Sometimes this means a showroom where you can look at different ranges and compare prices; sometimes it means an information centre where you can get professional and impartial advice.

THE BUILDING CENTRE, 26 Store Street, WC1 [636 – 5400].
Here is a permanent exhibition of 700 or so displays together with an information service on every aspect of building, maintaining and equipping the home. There are special advisory sections for heating and timber and the Gas and Electricity Councils are represented. Party visits for schools, colleges, clubs etc. can be arranged with the Education Officer. Opening hours: Monday to Wednesday, 9.30 a.m.–5.30 p.m.; Thursday, 9.30 a.m.–7 p.m.; Friday, 9.30 a.m.–5 p.m.

If you don't know anyone who can recommend a good builder, then, for small jobs (plumbing, electricity, minor alterations, etc.), select someone from the small ads. in your local paper. If they have actually spent money on advertising at least they are likely to turn up. For major jobs go for advice to:
MASTER BUILDERS' FEDERATION, 33 John Street, WC1 [242 – 7583].
This is the professional body of the building trade and will provide you with members' names.

THE DESIGN CENTRE, 28 Haymarket, SW1 [839 – 8000].
Exhibitions of the best in British design, the majority of which are home-centred. There is an index of products available to the public, with over 11,000 entries of well-designed modern consumer goods.

THE NATIONAL HEATING CENTRE, 34 Mortimer Street, W1 [580 – 3238].

This is the only independent advisory service on domestic heating in the country. There is a permanent exhibition and a library of leaflets available. A nominal charge of around £1, for consultations on individual heating problems, and £1 for answering a written inquiry is made, but no inquiries regarding heating can be dealt with on the telephone. They will also check estimates, charging 1 per cent of the total value of the estimate. A National Register of Heating Engineers is kept, backed by a two-year guarantee for full central heating jobs only.

WHICH? ADVICE CENTRE, 242 Kentish Town Road, NW5 [485 – 9939]. Open Tuesday, Wednesday, Friday, Saturday, 10 a.m.–6 p.m.; Thursday, 10 a.m.–1.30 p.m.

The services of the Advice Centre, run by the Consumers' Association, are free and available to all who call in. (They can't answer queries by phone or post.) You can wander round their display of goods and ask any questions you like. Before buying anything like a fridge, washing machine, record player, electric kettle or iron, you can get impartial pre-shopping information from one of the *Which?* advisers. If you like you can arrange an appointment by telephone, which is useful if you have a list of items to discuss. *Which?* don't recognize any one particular brand as an automatic 'best buy', but they help you to find out which is the best model to suit your individual needs and circumstances.

You can also catch up on back numbers of *Which?*, *Money Which?* and *Motoring Which?*, and there is a wide range of other consumer leaflets available. The *Which?* Advice Centre is particularly interested in contacting schools and will cooperate with teachers in planning special projects.

THE BRITISH CARPET CENTRE, Dorland House, 14–16 Lower Regent Street, SW1 [930 – 8711].

This is a showroom for the British woven-carpet industry, which means that Axminster and Wilton carpets only are displayed, not tufted ones. Over twenty-four top carpet manufacturers display their ranges here and there are over 3,000 samples all fully labelled together with approximate retail prices. You can't buy or order direct from the Centre, but in case of difficulty in obtaining what you've chosen, the manufacturer will provide a list of local retailers.

THE KITCHEN AND BATHROOM CENTRE, 22 Conduit Street, W1 [493 – 6822].

The Centre has a large display of units by leading manufacturers. They have a planning service and can supply a builder's name if required. Local authority improvement grants can be obtained in order to install bathrooms in old property. Your local town hall or Citizens' Advice Bureau will have leaflets about this.

THE LONDON BEDDING CENTRE, 26–7 Sloane Street, SW1 [584 – 1777].

This Centre shows and sells beds and bedding, including linen, on three floors. They deliver free of charge anywhere in Great Britain. There is a special shop within the main shop dealing specifically with export orders from foreign visitors.

Auctions

Many auctioneers hold regular sales of specialized collectors' items. These are always on show a day or two before the sale, and even if you don't attend the auction, it's worth a visit to the saleroom to look round and see a large collection all in one place. Catalogues are always available.

CHRISTIE MANSON AND WOODS, 8 King Street, SW1 [839 – 9060].

KNIGHT, FRANK AND RUTLEY, 20 Hanover Square, W1 [629 – 8171].

SOTHEBY & CO., 34 New Bond Street, W1 [493 – 7242].

The telephone directory (yellow pages) will give you information about smaller local auction rooms.

Secondhand Furniture

Most secondhand places will deliver. But usually they take cash only, no cheques, so make sure you've got sufficient money with you.

AUSTINS, 11–13 Peckham Rye, SE15 [639 – 3163]. Several floors of antiques and junk at varying prices.

JUNK CITY, Bell Street, NW1 [402 – 6723]. Furniture as well as cookers.

SECONDHAND CITY, Methodist Church, North End Road, W14 [385 – 7711]. Cheap solid furniture which you can often strip yourself.

THE SALVATION ARMY DEPOT, 124 Spa Road, SE16 [237 – 1107]. Open weekdays but Saturday is bargain day.

Home Flower Delivery

FOUR SEASONS FLOWER CLUB, 11 New Quebec Street, W1 [262 – 6611].

If you live in central London, the Club will deliver seasonal flowers to your home each week. The cost varies from 50p upwards a week with an annual subscription of 50p a year. To join send the subscription fee plus a remittance for four weeks' flowers to the Club and delivery will begin immediately. The Club also supplies, plants, and maintains window boxes.

Baby-sitters

There are a number of agencies who supply baby-sitters. They can very often supply home-helps and domestic cleaners as well. If you have found a reliable agency, and need domestic help, it is worth asking their advice.

UNIVERSAL AUNTS LTD, 36 Walpole Street, SW3 [730 – 9834].

Apart from baby-sitting, they will offer help in almost any situation you can think of, from exercising your dog to doing your packing or shopping.

BABYMINDERS, 126 Wigmore Street, W1 [935 – 3515].

BABY SITTERS UNLIMITED, 9 Ovington Street, SW3 [730 – 7778].

SOLVE YOUR PROBLEMS, 158a Old Brompton Road, SW5 [373 – 9344].

Lost Property

When you lose something in London, it is important to remember what you were doing or where you were going when you lost it,

and the date. You would be surprised how many people lost a
navy-blue umbrella on the Central Line during July.

Where lost	*Go (don't phone)*
Bus or tube	London Transport Lost Property Office, 200 Baker Street, NW1
Train	Main line terminus
Taxi	Lost Property Office, Penton Street, N1
Elsewhere	Local police station

Telephone Services

Emergencies. Ask for service required, fire, police,
ambulance or doctor   **999**

Telegrams. Inland telegrams, ships' telegrams and
inquiries   **190**
Overseas telegrams   **557**
Overseas telegrams inquiries   **559**

Express Messenger will deliver letters and parcels or
what you will during normal business hours. The
cost is 15p per mile travelled by the messenger from
his office to point of delivery. Ring your nearest
principal post office.

Alarm Calls. Book through the operator, before
10.30 p.m. if possible   **191**

Telephone breakdown   **151**

Directory inquiries (to trace subscribers' numbers
and other information for inland and Irish Republic)   **192**

Motoring information within 50 miles of London   **246 – 8021**

Weather forecast for South East England

London	246 – 8091
Essex coast	246 – 8096
Sussex coast	246 – 8097
Kent coast	246 – 8098
Thames valley	246 – 8090
Bedford area	246 – 8099

For other areas consult the telephone directory.
For personal advice on the weather call:
Meteorological Office, London Weather Centre   **836 – 4311**

Teletourist for the main events of the day in and around London

English	246 – 8041
French	246 – 8043
German	246 – 8045
Spanish	246 – 8047
Italian	246 – 8049

Test Match score available 8 a.m.–7 p.m. (not Sundays) during Test Matches   160

Financial Times Share Index is up-dated four times a day   246 – 8026

Dial-a-Disc has a different record from the week's top seven each night, 6 p.m.–8 a.m. (From 7 p.m. during Test Matches)   160

Recipe for the day   246 – 8071

Time Speaking Clock   123

Dial-a-Poem   836 – 2872

Bedtime Story can be dialled after 6 p.m.   246 – 8000

Greater London Information Service is a telephone inquiry service set up to provide information either about London or for people living in London. The hours are Monday to Friday, 9 a.m.–6 p.m. At other times there is a recording service and if you leave your name, telephone number or address, together with the query, they will get in touch with you the following day. (The telephone number is due to be changed in the near future, so watch the press for an announcement.)   928 – 0303

The *Daily Telegraph* bureau will give you information about most matters both topical and general. (9.30–5.30 Monday to Friday.)   353 – 4242

London Transport inquiries (if you can get through to this number you're lucky).   222 – 1234

HIRE SERVICES

HIRE SERVICE SHOPS, Head Office: Essex Road, Acton, W3 [992 – 0101]. (Branches in London and the Home Counties.)

This chain of hire shops supplies equipment to help build, paint, decorate and clean a house. They also hire out gardening tools, party and camping equipment, and many other things that most people only need temporarily, and therefore do not wish to buy.

If you are giving a party, remember that most off-licence wine shops will hire out glasses when you buy your drink, and many of them will supply beer, wines and spirits on a sale or return basis.

HARRODS, Knightsbridge, SW1 [730 – 1234].

Equipment for parties can be hired, such as china and glassware, cutlery, and all silverware used in catering – punch bowls, soup tureens, serving dishes, candlesticks, cake stands and so on.

Baby equipment

HARRODS, Knightsbridge, SW1 [730 – 1234].

Prams, pushchairs, cots, playpens, and high chairs can be hired.

DAVIES BABY CARRIAGES, 8 Hornton Street, W8 [937 – 4201].

Prams can be hired, but as demand exceeds supply, it is as well to book early.

BABY SCALE HIRE, 61 Lilford Road, SE5 [274 – 8762], and GUARDIAN BABY SCALES LTD, 45 Holloway Road N7 [602 – 6105].

Both these firms hire out baby scales and will deliver within the London area.

NAPPYLAND NAPPY LAUNDRY, 3 Hythe Road, NW10 [969 – 6456].

A nappy-washing service is provided, with collection and delivery either daily or three times a week, according to how much you feel like paying, and where you live. The daily service costs £1·50 a week, and allows you up to sixty nappies a week. The three-times-a-week service costs £1 a week, and allows fourteen nappies at each collection.

Back issues

DAWSON'S, Back Issues Department, Cannon House, Folkestone.

Dawson's will provide back numbers of periodicals – 'not women's magazines, of course, but most weeklies, monthlies and quarterlies'.

Bicycles

SAVILLE'S CYCLE STORES LTD, 99 Battersea Rise, SW11 [228 – 4279].

Bicycles may be hired. £1.25 is charged for the first week and then 12½p a day. A deposit of £5 is required plus proof of identity.

Camera hire

DIXONS, 27 Oxford Street, W1 [437 – 8811].

As well as doing camera repairs, Dixons has a wide selection of cameras for hire, ranging in price from £2–5 a week.

SAMUELSON FILM SERVICES LTD, 303–305 Cricklewood Broadway, NW2 [452 – 8090].

A wide range of cameras and camera equipment can be hired, including lighting, editing, underwater and projection equipment.

WALLACE HEATON LTD, 127 New Bond Street, W1 [629 – 7511].

Projectors and films can be hired. To hire any projector for an evening or longer you must pay a deposit and, in the winter, give at least one month's notice. The cost of hiring varies according to the model, but slide projectors cost from £2.10 to £4.20 with a £15–20 deposit, and cine-projectors from £3.15 for 8mm. (£6.30 with sound) to £4.20 for 16mm. (£10.50 with sound and a projectionist) with a £35–50 deposit. You can also hire a large variety of films at various prices varying between 65p for a short film to £2.50 for a feature film lasting, say, ninety minutes. Deposits for films are £3 per reel.

Camping equipment

BLACKS OF GREENOCK, Ruxley Corner, Sidcup, Kent [302 – 0211].

Specialists in camping-equipment hire. Send for their brochure.

TOWNSEND-THORESSEN CAR FERRIES, 199 Regent Street, W1 [734 – 4431].

A hire-service is run for their passengers. You collect and deliver the equipment at the port of departure.

Clothes for special occasions

MOSS BROS. LTD, Bedford Street, WC2 [240 – 4567].

Clothes can be hired for every conceivable formal occasion from a posh wedding to a garden party, including accessories like shoes, bags, stoles and jewellery. They also do ski-wear. Call seven days in advance.

TWENTIETH CENTURY FUR HIRERS LTD, 120 Wigmore Street, W1 [835 – 1444].

All their furs are covered by insurance so they want a reference. This can take some time to clear, so don't leave the arrangements till the last minute.

YOUNGS DRESS HIRE, 178–80 Wardour Street, W1 [437 – 4422].

Wedding clothes are their speciality. Call seven days in advance.

BRIDES BOUTIQUE AND HIRE DEPARTMENT, 7 Upper James Street, W1 [437 – 3363].

Specialists in providing complete outfits for brides, brides-maids and pages.

Ice cubes

ICE CUBES LTD, 49 Wales Farm Road, W3 [992 – 6822].

They will deliver a 25-lb. bag of ice cubes for 75p, and will also hire out insulated boxes for 25p a day. There is no delivery charge in the London area.

Jukebox hire

Jukeboxes can be hired from the Hire Service shops (see p. 191) for £10 a day in the week and £12 a day at weekends, as well as from the firms listed below.

NPB ENTERPRISES LTD, 205 Whittington Road, N22 [888 – 8996].

This firm hires jukeboxes (£13·65 a night), and pin-tables

and football-tables (£5 a night). They deliver and collect. For a Saturday booking collection is made on Monday, but charged for one evening. You should give a week or fortnight's notice.

JUKEBOX DISTRIBUTORS LTD, North Block, Cricklewood Trading Estate, Clairmont Road, NW2 [450 – 5221].

The charge for a jukebox is £15·75 an evening within the London area, and they will quote for delivery further out. You should give at least a week's notice for a booking.

For parties and fund-raising

BARNUMS (Carnival Novelties) Ltd, 67 Hammersmith Road, W14 [602 – 1211].

With great gusto Barnums hire and sell a vast variety of things like masks, marquees, theatrical costumes, stage props, dance floors, balloons, prizes, party games – anything you can name in what one might call the 'have-a-good-time business'. Their spokesman said, 'If we haven't got it, we'll always try to get it.'

A. TOMASSO AND SON, 4a The Broadway, N14 [886 – 4198].

Barrel-organs can be hired by the day, at from £2 to £5 according to the event.

Housemoving

You might find it more economical to get the removal men with a pantechnicon to move the double bed and the grand piano, but hire a van for the books, records and goldfish.

HERTZ RENT-A-VAN, 1 Drummond Crescent, NW1 [387 – 9075].

Vans with or without a driver.

TAXI-TRUCKS TRANSPORT, 22a South Hill Park Gardens, NW3 [794 – 0444].

Also look at local newsagents' boards for local van-owners.

Refrigerators

Prices vary according to the size of the model.

REFRIGERATOR RENTALS, Knightsbridge House, 197 Knightsbridge, SW7 [584 – 3221].

H. J. HOUGH, 81 Kensington Church Street, W8 [937 – 3065]. As well as hiring they also do repairs.

Scooter hire

SCOOT-ALONG LTD, 33 Old Kent Road, SE11 [703 – 3570].

This firm hires motor scooters and mopeds. You must have a licence or provisional licence. The hire charges are £1.50 per day, £7 a week and £25 for 31 days with a deposit of £15–20 for a Lambretta, and lower scales for mopeds. They run a three-month re-purchase scheme for secondhand machines.

SCOOTER-HIRE SERVICE, 61 Tottenham Lane, N8 [340 – 0333].

Scooters can be hired for £8 a week with 400 miles of free mileage. A deposit of £15 is required.

Sewing machines

SEW FASHIONS LTD, 130 Ewell Road, Surbiton [399 – 0111].

All well-known makes of sewing machine can be hired. You must give two to three days' advance warning. Hire charges are £1.50 per week, which includes delivery and collection, service and repairs. A deposit of £5 is required for a short hire, otherwise the fee is payable in advance.

SEWING MACHINES SALE AND HIRE, 513 Hackney Road, E2 [739 – 7954].

Sewing machines can be hired for 75p a week plus a delivery and installation charge of £5. The firm also hires out industrial sewing machines.

Tape-recorder hire

MAGNEGRAPH RECORDING CO. LTD, 1 Hanway Place, W1 [580 – 2156].

Ring in advance so that the correct model can be got ready for you to collect. Prices vary according to size from 62½p a day (£2·10 a week) for a portable model, to £2·50 a day (£10·50 a week) for the most expensive. A deposit of from £10 to £25 must be paid when you collect.

Theatrical props

CAPE OF CHISWICK, 85 Crouch Hill, N8 [272 – 4654].

Ring for an appointment to arrange for the hire of stage scenery, draperies and backcloths.

CAVALCADE, 28 The Green, Twickenham [894 – 9800].

Cavalcade hires costumes for theatricals and fancy dress. They have period costumes from medieval to space age, foreign costumes and some animal suits. The hire charge for a costume with its accessories is about £2 an evening. Ring for an appointment for a fitting about two to three weeks before you want the costume. It will then be sewn, cleaned and packed for collection.

RANK STRAND ELECTRIC LTD, 250 Kennington Lane, SE11 [735 – 7811].

They hire stage-lighting equipment and decorative lighting – 'chandeliers for receptions and things like that'.

Typewriter hire

ACTON TYPEWRITER CO. LTD, 47 Churchfield Road, W3 [992 – 0469].

Delivery and collection charges are included in hire rates which run from £3 per week for a manual typewriter to £10 per week or £24 per month for an electric typewriter.

INDEX